P.

The Map of Me

The Map of Me

Fourteen True Tales of
Mixed-Heritage Experience

PENGUIN BOOKS

305.8
MAP

PENGUIN BOOKS

Published by the Penguin Group
Penguin Books Ltd, 80 Strand, London WC2R ORL, England
Penguin Group (USA), Inc., 375 Hudson Street, New York, New York 10014, USA
Penguin Group (Canada), 90 Eglinton Avenue East, Suite 700, Toronto, Ontario, Canada M4P 2Y3
(a division of Pearson Penguin Canada Inc.)
Penguin Ireland, 25 St Stephen's Green, Dublin 2, Ireland (a division of Penguin Books Ltd)
Penguin Group (Australia), 250 Camberwell Road, Camberwell, Victoria 3124, Australia
(a division of Pearson Australia Group Pty Ltd)
Penguin Books India Pvt Ltd, 11 Community Centre, Panchsheel Park, New Delhi – 110 017, India
Penguin Group (NZ), 67 Apollo Drive, Rosedale, North Shore 0632, New Zealand
(a division of Pearson New Zealand Ltd)
Penguin Books (South Africa) (Pty) Ltd, 24 Sturdee Avenue,
Rosebank, Johannesburg 2196, South Africa

Penguin Books Ltd, Registered Offices: 80 Strand, London WC2R ORL, England

www.penguin.com

First published 2008
1

Set in Monotype Dante
Typeset by Rowland Phototypesetting Ltd, Bury St Edmunds, Suffolk
Printed in England by Clays Ltd, St Ives plc

ISBN: 978-0-141-03892-6

www.greenpenguin.co.uk

Penguin Books is committed to a sustainable future
for our business, our readers and our planet.
The book in your hands is made from paper
certified by the Forest Stewardship Council.

Contents

Contents

The Inadvertent Creation of a Soul Sister

Rounke Coker

'Owwwwww!'

'*Pele.*' (Sorry.)

'OOOUUCH!! That hurts!'

'Sorry, dear . . . Your hair tangles so easily!'

It was 5.30 in the morning, the sun was racing up over the horizon and the birds in the pink apple tree were tweeting into wakefulness. Street vendors could already be heard crying out for custom – '*Ogi re!*' (Corn pap), '*Ogede O!*' (Plantains!) – and there was incessant honking of bulb horns by newspaper sellers shouting, '*Daily Times! Nigerian Tribune! Daily Sketch!* Get your papers here!' Bus conductors added to the racket as they roared past in Volkswagen Kombis, yelling, '*Eko-Eko-Eko O!*' (Lagos-Lagos-Lagos!). The whole world, it seemed, was busy preparing for a day's work in the largest black African city in the world.

With the help of copious amounts of baby oil, Mother finally combed out the tangles in my hair and made a long central parting. She rapidly wove two long plaits, which she knotted together at their ends. This was to prevent me whipping my own face with

3

them whenever I turned my nine-year-old head round fast. The whole hair thing took about half an hour. It was different for Mother. She just brushed her long brunette hair, tucked it into a French roll, stuck in a few hairpins and grips, and hey presto! It took only a few minutes. Even my younger brother, Bolaji, merely had a comb dragged through his short curls for a few seconds, usually at the last minute before leaving home. At seven years old, he wasn't much concerned about his hair yet; that would come much later on. Father's hair never changed from its neatly barbered black nap, with parting shaved into one side.

We were normally woken at 5.00 in the morning to bathe and dress for school. That ungodly hour ensured that we left the house no later than 6.00, when we would join the millions making their way on foot, bicycles and motorcycles, in cars and buses, out of the suburbs to schools, factories, offices and places of business. It was 1972 and Nigeria would soon become the eighth-largest crude oil producer in the world. One outcome of this was an explosion in vehicle ownership. Bolaji and I spent hours in a chauffeured car supplied by Father's Ministry of Establishments, crawling across the city from Suru-lere, where we lived, to Akoka, where our school was located in the grounds of the University of Lagos – a distance of maybe six miles. But we would normally arrive in time for assembly at 8.00, unless overnight rain or a road accident closed a major route, or there had been a coup, in which case no school!

'I really want to cut my hair, Mummy. It would be much easier to comb in the mornings,' I begged, resuming an age-old debate.

'But darling, how would you take care of it? This hair just won't hold thread or cornrows!' replied Mother sympathetically.

Sadly, this was true. Auntie 'Wunmi had tried during the summer holidays. I think she felt that Mother was too English and not open enough to the Yoruba way of doing things, particularly in the matter of hair. It was often this way with us – we few, we not completely Nigerian few. Friends and neighbours – even complete strangers – sometimes openly voiced their doubts about this Englishwoman's ability to cope with life in Nigeria. It was commonplace for people to think she didn't know how to cook *ogbona* (a type of soup) or wear *iro* and *buba* (wrapper and blouse). In fact, my only complaint with Mother's food was that there wasn't enough *ata* (pepper) in it – we children had holidayed too often with Mama Shalewa, an older sister of Father's, whose love of *ata* was legendary. And I didn't blame Mother for eschewing Yoruba dress, as, unlike every other Nigerian woman, she was completely flat – possibly even concave – in the region of her gluteus maximus. The *iro* looked baggy and badly tied on her. She did

5

not have the 'African asset' required to carry one in the correct manner, with an appreciable roundness of form and a pronounced and rhythmic sway. But what did it matter, when her Yoruba husband was a civil servant who wore handmade suits (they had to be handmade, he said, to accommodate the 'African asset') and long-sleeved shirts every day? With a double-knot tie and cufflinks!

Yet Auntie 'Wunmi had meant well. I had been quite happy to let her experiment. She had sat me down on a mat between her thighs, combed my hair with an Afro comb – which was much better than the comb Mother used – and then divided it into four sections. She had gathered a bunch of hair in one hand and then whipped lengths of black thread rapidly around it, to encase it in a tight, even wrapping of close-set thread. She had then tried to bend each threaded plait tastefully, to create 'style' in the hair – but that was a step too far; my hair was just too soft. Nevertheless, we had both been pleased with the final result. It had felt like I was carrying a ton of scaffolding on my head, but I looked more like any other Nigerian girl than I had ever done with two plaits down my back.

Then Bolaji and I had gone out to play – football, I think it was – and within the hour disaster had struck. The thread had began to unravel and my hair had begun to blow loose in the breeze. Poor Auntie

'Wunmi! She had been so put out! Mother had looked rather smug, but perhaps I just imagined it. The next experiment was with cornrowing – just the common *shuku* style, weaving rows from the base of the head to the crown and forming a circular crest at the top of the head with the ends of the plaits. Same result.

'But can't I just have it short and loose, like Danmola's hair?' I pleaded in a wheedling tone, twisting the hem of my green striped uniform with anxious fingers.

Danmola Gbadamosi had a German mother and Yoruba father, and her hair was nearly straight. She sported a no-nonsense mop that required regular trimming (usually on a Saturday morning with her mother's sewing shears), but her mornings were not spent in a painful fog of untangling and plaiting.

'But then you'd indeed look *very* different from all your friends at school, wouldn't you?' Mother pointed out. 'Danmola still complains about people staring at her, doesn't she?'

She knew that this was one of my 'issues' with my genetic inheritance. I longed to look like everyone else, to be able to 'sculpt' my hair like all the other girls ('*Eko* Bridge' being the latest fashion) and wear colours like bright red without looking sunburnt. Indeed, not to suffer sunburn itself would have been great! But, most of all, not to attract attention all the time, every blessed minute of the day. To be able to be naughty in public without everyone knowing whose daughter you were – now, that would have been priceless.

When I first started at this school, the other children had openly discussed my ancestry in front of me – as if I wasn't there.

'I think she's from China!' said a boy who, I later learned was named Bode.

'No, she's Arab. Aren't you?' asked a girl named Funmi, rounding on me.

Before I could protest, another boy called Lanre said, 'No o! I'm telling you, she's South African! I've seen them on the television.'

It went on in this vein for quite some time, until the execrable Bode said to me, 'Ah! Wait! I know where you're from. You're Brazilian, aren't you?'

They wouldn't believe that Father was Nigerian and a Yoruba man to boot, until Speech Day nine months later, which he was forced to attend because I was to be presented with the prize for best handwriting. Bode's face was a treat when he saw his dad and my dad exchange greetings like old friends – in Yoruba! They'd grown up in the same part of Lagos Island.

'But it wouldn't hurt so much . . . and you wouldn't have to plait it every day!' I had suddenly hit on a compelling argument, for Mother went quiet.

'I'll see what your father thinks,' she said eventually.

'What's Daddy got to do with it?' I moaned rather rudely, as I rose from the chair and began to pack my satchel. *He* didn't have hair like this and *he* didn't plait it, so why was it necessary to consult him?

'You know what your father thinks about appearance and presentation,' said Mother firmly, pulling loose hair out of the comb and throwing it into the waste basket.

Father was a stickler for appearances. Jeans were forbidden, make-up was an abomination on an unmarried woman and anything more than two inches above the knee was out of the question. He also had a thing about hair and couldn't stand to see strands of it clogging plugholes, left in combs, stuck on bars of soap or drifting across the terrazzo floor to line the bottom of the skirting boards. In my heart, I knew that shorter hair wouldn't solve the problem of 'difference', but at least mornings wouldn't be such a nuisance. And I could do my hair myself – 'comb and go'!

I don't know what she said to him, but on a Saturday mid-morning a few weeks later Mother and I made our way to Lovemore Cole's salon. It was located on McEwen Street in Yaba, opposite Domino Stores. I'd never been to a proper hairdresser's before, so I was doubly excited at the prospect of trouble-free, stylishly cut hair and the certainty of more relaxed mornings to come. For ever! Mr Cole was a man of slim build and average height. His own hair was low-cut and normal-looking. But he was dressed in tight, colourfully striped trousers with large bell-bottoms and his beige shirt was figure-hugging and buttoned only halfway up, so you could see his chest. I was quietly delighted with his garb, as I equated it with someone who was hip, whose sense of style would mean my new haircut would be fashionable. To my eyes, he dressed like James Brown, whose hit 'Say It Loud (I'm Black and I'm Proud)' – or, as Mother teased after she heard me singing outside the kitchen, 'Say It Loud, I'm Black and White' – had recently swept Nigeria. Mr Cole's appearance made Mother feel uncomfortable. She went all quiet and her lips suddenly became thinner, which was a sign that she was not happy and might change her mind. I began to pray *hard*: *Please, God! Please, God! Let it just happen*.

Mr Cole asked what we would like. However, when Mother let it be known that we required a cut to form a short mop, Mr Cole's response made my heart sink.

'What! Why do you want to cut this hair, madam – it's so beautiful!' he exclaimed disbelievingly, looking at my English mother as if she was crazed and guilty of child abuse.

Mother patiently explained the palaver we went through every morning and how attempts to Nigerianize the hair had failed. But Mr Cole persisted for some time in extolling the virtues of my hair and insisting that it would be a crime to cut any of it off. In the end, when Mother threatened to take our business elsewhere, he consented to do what we wanted. But as he unravelled my plaits, combed out my hair and began to snip it off, he kept up a running commentary on how lovely it was, 'so long and straight', 'so soft and pliable', 'what a pity' it was and how 'people would pay a *fortune* to have hair like this'. They're welcome to it, I thought to myself.

In the end, we got what we wanted – and Mr Cole did a good job. The cut produced a mop of balanced, straight edges with wavy ends that framed my face. He asked me to comb it out, to make sure it was easy for me to do. I was thoroughly delighted and my voice rose several octaves with pleasure as I thanked him. It was now early afternoon and Mother was relieved it was all over, though she did seem to look slightly regretfully at the hanks of hair on the floor. Anyway, I thought, it's too late now. Yippeeee!

We stopped on the way home for some provisions at Sabo Market nearby. It was her preferred market, as she had shopped there since coming to Nigeria to marry Father in 1960. She was known to many of its market women and had learned through bantering with them a *little* bit about how to strike a bargain African-style. Being white, she was highly visible and the market women could see profit coming from a mile off, so they were very welcoming and obliging. I tagged along behind, feeling the hot breeze blow through my hair and enjoying the freeness of the mop. No tightness on my scalp, no painful combing out of knots, no painful partings with the tooth of a comb! No more being tied to the swing or plait-ends being dipped in the inkpot of the desk behind me in class!

An anonymous horde of children of the market women began their familiar chant, directed at ex-patriates and their progeny:

'*Oyinbo* (white person) *pehpeh* (pepper),
If you eatee pehpeh,
You go yellow moh (more), *moh!*
Oyinbo pehpeh,
If you eatee . . .'

Today, I didn't care. I was cool, calm and collected. Nothing could dampen my mood. Besides, as soon as Mother's back was turned, I planned to retaliate with a chant I'd recently honed to perfection with Danmola's help. It described the increase of flatulence in people who eat sugar, which was a rare treat for these children. Regrettably, the opportunity did not arise. The market women kept asking Mother who I was, so changed was my appearance – the same thing had happened the year before, when I had started wearing glasses. Mother laughingly told them about my haircut and the market women were horrified. I was urged to grow my hair back with all possible speed, because '*Ko da ra ra! –* 'e no good ataaalll!'

On the journey back home, Mother chewed her lips and tried to run down any motorcyclist who got in her way – sure signs that she was nervous and irritated. I was absolutely determined, though, that there would be no growing back of the hair, even if I had to trim it myself with secateurs! As soon as we were parked outside our garage, I raced into the living room to show Father my hair, sure of his joy at my new-found light-headedness. Mother lagged far behind, supervising the apparently complicated unloading of her small amount of shopping.

'Daddy, Daddy! Daddy, look at my hair! It's soooo nice! We went to McEwen Street and Lovemore Cole. He was wearing *kokose* ('keep Lagos clean': slang for floor-sweeping flares), Daddy, and he ... Daddy?'

Father looked up from his newspaper and gazed at me as if he'd never seen me before. Then he said gravely, 'Yes, dear,' rose, went upstairs and shut himself away. Ooops, not a good time, I thought –

problems at his office sometimes made him a bit distanced and short-tempered. Thinking little more of it, I raced off to boast to friends next door, passing Mother on the way . . . still supervising the unloading of her shopping.

Many years passed before Mother told me, over a midnight snack of fried chicken and buttered bread, how she had found Father lamenting the loss of his 'little princess'. Now in my twenties, I felt no sympathy for him – and I wouldn't have had as a nine-year-old either, though I might not have been able to articulate it with such delicacy at that young age.

'So he had a European image of his little girl, did he? Ah-ah! How unrealistic can you get?' I exclaimed.

Father had no idea about being of mixed ethnicity or about growing up in the 1970s. He was not equipped to handle the stresses and strains that Bolaji and I had to confront – he lacked the emotional and psychological capacity to understand, never mind solve, the conundrums and conflicts that arose from being black *and* white. He could not understand, for example, why it drove me incoherent with rage to be addressed as 'Yellow!' by people in the street who thought they were being complimentary. And I never could stand that colour, yellow, on walls, in flowers, on clothes . . . Mother saw more of what went on – the snide remarks, the exclusions, the fact that we were considered fair game for everybody's inaccurate observations – but did not really know how to handle it. She seemed to think that being of mixed ethnicity in Nigeria was the same as being white in Nigeria. This was unhelpful: in those days white people in Nigeria were taken seriously as business people, professionals, spies or simply rich and powerful. People of mixed race – and they were mostly children at that time – were often seen as exotica to be envied or toyed with. The words 'race' and 'racism' were never mentioned in our house. Father just seemed to think that 'Character maketh the man!' Hnnh! That was the second unfought battle – his unshakeable belief in the lesser capabilities of women. No wonder I later on tried to spend as much time as possible in the UK! At least there, women's rights were up for discussion, if not wholly respected, and the racism was such that we minorities were all black together ... more or less ... most of the time!

I helped myself to the chicken skin that Mother was leaving on the side of her plate.

'Is that why you put up with the daily plaiting for so long?' I asked her.

She nodded. 'You have to understand, Rounke.* All parents worry about their children growing up – especially their daughters.'

* 'Rounke' is the traditional spelling of this name; the modern version is spelt 'Ronke'. It has a variety of prefixes, depending on family preferences.

'Ehn ehn!' I protested. 'All that "You can't wear jeans", "You can't use nail varnish"! That was all anti-European, yet he wanted me to keep looking as *oyinbo* as possible with long hair!'

I was *annoyed* with that man. It was one thing to be an idealist or a hopeless romantic; quite another to engender in his own child a profound confusion about her identity simply because of his private passions!

'As for worrying about "growing up",' I continued, 'he should be pleased I haven't presented him with fatherless grandchildren, then, shouldn't he?'

Unwanted pregnancy was my parents' greatest fear.

'Next to *that*, "hair" is a small thing!' I mumbled through my next mouthful. The chicken skin was well seasoned and I could taste the groundnuts in the groundnut oil it had been fried in.

'Ah! Yeees,' said Mother softly, and turned to pouring tea into her cup.

'*What*?' I demanded. 'Wha-a-a-at?'

'Mmmph ... He's just mentioned once or twice lately ... how nice it would be to have grandchildren ... With,' she added hastily, 'a son-in-law, of course!'

I sighed deeply and looked at Mother over the top of my glasses, to let her know that I was serious.

'There are times when I really wonder if he lives in the same time-space continuum as the rest of us,' I muttered through clenched teeth. 'Tell Daddy *not* to hold his breath and to be grateful for small mercies! At least it was only my hair that changed!'

'Aaaaah, but it wasn't just the hair *that day*, was it?'

We burst out laughing heartily.

For, a very short time after the haircut, fate struck a major blow. It was the next afternoon or the one after that, when getting ready for an outing, I dressed up and began to comb the new hair. Only it wouldn't cooperate. It resolutely refused to comb into a mop. It was curlier than ever and, for the first time in my life, was actually *standing up*. Corkscrews of hair were pointing straight up at the ceiling. Not understanding what was happening, I went to my parents' room and borrowed Mother's brush. But every time I stopped brushing, my hair would slowly rise again. Panic set in.

'MUMMY! Come QUICK! Something's WROOONG!'

Mother took one look at me and my disobedient hair and sighed deeply.

We returned to Lovemore Cole's salon first thing the next morning. He was shocked at my appearance and, after examining my hair minutely, announced that the only solution was to shape it into an Afro. My heart leapt! I lowered my eyes so that Mother would not see the suddenly blazing hope in my eyes and feel duty-bound to put it out. She took some

17

convincing. Mr Cole warned that the only way to keep it lying down, now that we had gone against his initial advice of not cutting it, would be to use hair-straightening products regularly – something that both Mother and Father were implacably opposed to. So Mr Cole spent the next hour trimming my hair into a real, genuine, bona fide, solid-gold, black American-style Afro! It was beyond my wildest dreams. It had never entered my head to imagine an Afro, because it was so obviously not what well-brought-up girls were allowed to have. It would have been ruthlessly vetoed at the first mention – and the first rule of handling difficult parents was *let the idea come from them*, preferably when there was no longer any alternative. Now, here I was, owner of the most-sought-after hairstyle in the whole of Africa. I was ecstatic! I was hip! I was happening! I was up to the minute! I was black *and* white *and* most definitely *proud*! Poor old Father would just have to live with it. Look out, world! Miss Morounke Olugbaike Adetokubo Coker had *landed* – oh yeah!

I finally turned up for class as our teacher, Mrs Timehin, was expounding on the evils of the trans-atlantic slave trade, with her back to the door. My fellow pupils were all facing her and so had a clear view of my entry and I, of course, was smiling fit to burst. Everyone's jaw dropped, causing Mrs Timehin to stop in mid-flow, turn around and nearly have a heart attack. She actually clutched her chest and asked faintly whether I was trying to kill her.

'What on earth have you done to yourself, Rounke?' she demanded crossly.

I apologized for being late and ostentatiously emptied my satchel, looking for the explanatory note Mother had written, making sure everyone got an eyeful of my new wooden Afro comb with its extraordinarily long teeth, large handle and funky indigo-coloured squiggles dyed all over it.

'You look quite different,' remarked Mrs Timehin drily, after she'd calmed down and read the note.

'Thank you, Ma,' I replied smugly, head swelling even more as I made my way to my desk at the back of the classroom.

Then Bode leaned over and whispered to Lanre in the next row, apparently continuing the old argument, 'See? She's Michael Jackson's sister!'

Asian Invisible

Julia Bohanna

Other children had boring parents. But I had two film stars: my father a Brummie John Wayne, with his beloved faded jeans and lumbering cowboy walk, my mother all Bollywood ebony hair and olive skin. The dull families had parents who looked more like stiff bookends than mine. In the early 1970s we lived in a small market town and I had never seen another mixed marriage. To the locals, coloured skin was exotic, something that exercised their lips into a big fat 'O'. There was my six-foot-tall, whey-faced father with a tiny but shapely foreign woman. My friends' mothers were neat, blonde or head to toe in Marks & Spencer. Mine was all fiery and beautiful, but ultimately *different*.

When very young, I never questioned that no one mentioned India at home. I realized slowly that my mother and all her brothers were truly trying to be anglicized, to be invisible in a society that was at that time particularly suspicious of and disrespectful to Asians. She was pale enough to get away with the camouflage: some mistook her for Portuguese, even Italian or Greek. I found out later that we did also have some Portuguese blood to add to the mix, as well as Dutch – a result of connections with Goa and the Dutch East India Company. We even had pirates as ancestors. My mother's three daughters had only the raisin-dark eyes and hair to whisper clues of our heritage.

I was jealous of my mother's shiny black hair. She used to pay me to pluck out the grey. I was irritated that we had all inherited my father's pale skin. My Asian pigment came out in freckles, which were dotted on my nose every summer like foxing on an old mirror. After those had appeared, I would tan quite easily. But my mother had a beauty spot on her forehead in the exact place that a Hindu's bindi might have been; she always tried to cover it up with foundation, but you could still see the raised dot.

India was stamped on her whether she liked it or not.

The revelation of our history came at the same time as my hormones. I discovered a photograph album with pages of elegant dark-skinned people in it. There were my uncles as children and my mother holding a strange lady's hand.

'That was my ayah,' she told me. 'She was the one who accompanied me to convent school in Ajmer, where we were told by the nuns that there was a giant cobra and his mate living in one of the outbuildings.'

The serpents of Ajmer seemed like a fantastical story. My father's childhood had been adventures by canals or playing jokes on teachers. But this was glamour, intrigue, fear.

'It was only to make us stay in line,' she continued. 'Ensure that no one wandered off. But I was small and scared. Tigers never frightened me, but snakes and scorpions did. Every night before we went to sleep we had to check our beds for them. Then our slippers in the morning.'

I liked the saris worn by the women in the pictures; the photographs were black and white, so I had to imagine the rainbow colours. A lot held my imagination: there had been servants who cleaned my grandfather's shoes after he returned from tiger- and wolf-hunting with the maharaja. When I saw a picture of my grandfather, who had died when I was quite young, I fell in love. He was beautiful, dressed in cricket whites. Another film star.

My mother puzzled me, because she closed the album as if it should all be forgotten, kept in the past. I wanted to tell everyone these stories, make them realize that I was special, even aristocratic. I went to a Catholic school as well, but there were no snakes, just nuns who looked like hooded cobras them-selves as they slithered around corners and caught us out when we were late for class. It took me a very long time to learn that being Catholic in India had been unusual, another complicated aspect of our family.

'If anyone asks your nationality,' my mother said, 'you say British or *none of your damn business.*'

When an art teacher got the class to draw me because I had an 'interesting face' my mother marched into the school and confronted him. Did interesting mean foreign, conspicuous? She took umbrage at a lot of things that were not meant to offend; she was sensitive to being noticed. When my father's relatives visited they were very laid-back, with their lovely comedy accents; my uncle's idea of exotic food was pearl barley. They brought Black Country magazines that had cartoons about faggots and were written in dialect that was difficult to understand. I liked faggots and tripe as little as the foul and bitter lime pickle my Indian grandmother tried to spoon-feed me. The Brummies were kind and funny, but when relatives from both sides were together the combination was a strange one. I was the silent, observant child watching the two cultures mix and meld. To imagine that I was the result of this odd soup of nationalities was exciting. My Brummie cousin had a thick blond moustache, a Bentley and a boa constrictor. He played in a band and had a lot of fun in life. My brown uncles talked about their children following them into medicine, dentistry or medical research, as if there was no other choice for their lives.

Neither group truly understood the other's ambitions.

Back then, small towns gave most foreign people nicknames, the majority of them uncomplimentary. One blond, bulbous-headed boy called me Tutankhamun at school, probably because I broke the rules and wore thick black kohl around my eyes to look mysterious. Some laughed too when I told them my grandparents' Brummie names: Fanny and Cyril. So I was teased about both sides of the family.

Even more ignorant were the few unimaginative people who sensed I was different and called out, 'Paki.'

'If you have to speak to them at all, tell them that their geography is rubbish,' was my mother's advice. But I could see that she was hurt. 'Their history too. India and Pakistan haven't been friends since the 1947 partition.'

The partition of India was a particularly raw subject for our family. It had made them fearful. They had left India soon after the assassination of Gandhi in 1948, leaving all their wealth and property to the war profiteers. My mother was barely eleven but remembered hearing the news on the radio and then the panic that there would be further anarchy, bloodshed. It seemed the end of everything, India's Twin Towers. They went from respected rich Indians to poor asylum seekers, arriving in a country where 'No blacks, no dogs, no Irish' was a sign posted proudly in many windows.

No wonder my mother wanted to be a ghost.

Teenage anger hit me hard. Why couldn't I express myself openly and be proud of my ancestry? Why should I fade into the background? I would have loved to walk down the high street wrapped sensuously in a royal-purple sari flecked with gold thread. In the absence of that and to the horror of my parents, I became a punk and wore black bondage trousers with ugly zips like snarling mouths, then dyed my hair unearthly colours. I developed attitude, relishing the individualism and, better still, the fact that I had very different parents from all of my friends. I was never even scared of the tough-talking racist skinheads who regularly leaned their red braces on pigeon-stained benches in the middle of town. They spent hours smoking scruffy roll-ups and pretending to trip up elderly ladies. I recognized some of them from school and they would nod a greeting. I was a foreigner they knew, so that was all right.

Actually, *I* was all right.

It was much later, after I'd gone through my crisis of identity and come out quite defiant but happy, that I began to proudly tell people about my heritage. I went to London and there at last was a city of all shades, all languages. An urban paint chart. City people were interested generally in my funny back-ground, not hostile. They had culture mixes of their own.

The ultimate rebellion for the invisible Asian was when my daughter was born in 1997.

I called her India.

Growing up on Lard

Tina Maisie Chan Freeth

I grew up in Birmingham to English (read 'white') parents who loved me dearly but gave me steak and kidney pies to eat instead of rice. Not that they needed to give me the staple food of my ancestors, but I have concluded that my lack of 'Chineseness' is in direct proportion to the shortage of rice I ate as a child. Have to blame something, right? I could not blame the blessed souls who had chosen to adopt me, as rice just was not part of their daily diet, and I could not hold my biological parents responsible for wanting to give me to someone else to bring up. Perhaps I was just a baby who looked like she should not eat too much rice. I cannot really say. All I know is that our chips were cooked in lard.

The other Chinese kids at school (all two of them), their parents owned takeaways and, of course, they had rice there. I imagined hills of white rice behind the kitchen door, cooked and steaming like the romantic mists of the Far East I had seen on TV. Obviously, they would have had egg fried rice in abundance, shaken and coated with the love and affection that soy sauce brings to Chinese cuisine. A

Chinese kitchen without soy sauce is like a French kitchen without butter, or a British kitchen without ketchup. Of course, Chinese takeaways also had chips for those British people who did not want rice with their sweet and sour pork. Did they also cook their chips in lard? Had the Chinese who resided in those takeaways ever had a fish finger or chicken Kiev? Can my 'Britishness' be attributed to the amount of fish fingers I ate with tomato sauce on a 'piece' of buttered Mother's Pride white bread?

I remember the packed lunches I would take to primary school every day. They consisted of roast chicken (which had been cooked on the Sunday especially for me) on bread, a packet of Cheesy Snaps and a can of orange Tango. I would expertly and with technical precision place two and a half Snaps on one triangular sandwich. To this day, many years later, I can still appreciate the beauty that is a crisp sarnie. The crunching sound made by every purposeful bite and the wonderful textures of my hybrid sandwich made my taste buds stand on end, as if saluting my inventive revolt against the school dinners that I detested. The realization that my adapted masterpiece held within its breaded walls a burst of faux-cheese flavouring made my heart swell with love. I ate this every day for years, sitting on the plastic green chair in the dining hall, making sure I ate my crusts. Mum would say, 'Come on, Bab.

Eat your crusts like a good girl. They'll make your hair curly.' She lied. Perhaps it only curls if you are white. We Chinese are well known for our naturally straight hair and, no matter how many crusts I ate, I was never going to be the Chinese Shirley Temple.

I would always watch with mild amusement when both of my parents spread dripping on to a 'piece': white pig fat would sit precariously in a lump where Mum could not be bothered to distribute it evenly, the amber jelly-like substance sitting in between, the poor person's snack. My dad's shining example of a ready meal in a pre-microwave era was an Oxo cube drowned in boiling water. The brown murky depths reminded me of the local canals, with their shopping trolleys and rusted bicycles. Into this cheap boiling concoction he would submerge roughly ripped pieces of sliced white bread. What terror it must have been to be that bread, scalded by dirty brown liquid and then stuffed into a mouth where no teeth resided (due to a massive intake of sugar at a young age), to be chomped and mauled by a set of hard gums.

Is there such a person as a food psychoanalyst, a Captain Birdseye Freud or a Sarah Lee Jung? If there is, I am sure they would lay me down on their black leather couch and I would spill my repressed secrets like molten Cheddar cheese oozing furiously from the triangular pockets of a Breville toasted sandwich, regurgitating my sordid past of fry-ups and bubble and squeak. I would confess my early addiction to Bernard Matthews's Chicken Drummers and Findus Crispy Pancakes, grease bleeding from their golden outer covering. I would guiltily reveal my love of stew and dumplings, the animal-fat content of which turned me into a human sausage roll. I was ten stone when I was ten years old.

Bacon and egg sandwiches were a regular fix. If I had been a particularly good girl I was given a special 'triple decker', a three-layered sandwich, one of which alone would have raised my body-fat percentage to thirty-five. Yes, yes, I can smell the odours of my youth. They haunt me like the piercing beep-beep sound of the smoke alarm when Mum burned the chips. My Great British breakfast childhood. My mixed-grill heritage.

There was no problem trying to coax me to eat, like there is with some kids. My younger foster brother had to be prodded and coerced. Normal chicken soup was transformed by name alone to the more heroic 'Superman Soup' and only then would he take one spoonful. However, that was never the case for me. I ate and ate. Fondly nicknamed 'the human rubbish bin' by my mum, who thought I had insides like a Hoover. I just sucked up all remaining food from everyone's plates. 'Waste not, want not' was the motto in our house. I was conscientious even back then: I knew there were children starving in

Africa, so to leave one baked bean on my plate would have been sacrilege. Nothing was left over, nothing forgotten. We were not a rich family, renting from the council, so no flat above a takeaway for me. But I never felt we were one of those families who went without. We had too much. The cupboards were always overflowing with food. At the back of every one, it was guaranteed that there would be an out-of-date packet of blancmange and a jar of pickled onions from some Christmas hamper way back in the late 1970s.

There was a time when I tried to be more 'Chinese'. I would watch kung fu movies and of course ordered prawn crackers with my takeaways. I would tell the kids at school that Jackie Chan was my father. I was confused about whether I was Chinese or British. I looked Chinese and occasionally my older white brother would call me 'Chink' affectionately, but maybe I just did not eat the rice in the right way. I used to scoop it into my prawn cracker, which I used like a spoon. Of course, I would then eat the makeshift spoon and that is just not Chinese.

Sometimes we ate out at fancy Chinese restaurants, when the biological parents of the other Chinese kids my parents fostered came to visit. I would be put to the Chinese 'test of authenticity': using the dreaded chopsticks. I recall one time at a restaurant in Chinatown how I flatly refused and, in my defence, proclaimed how useless they were. 'I can get more in my mouth with a spoon!' I shouted. I just could not see the point of trying to get food into my mouth with two long sticks with tiny ends. Where was the logic in chopsticks? Which fool had invented this finicky mechanism of click-clacking two sticks together to use as eating utensils? The truth was that I failed the test. I could not use them, did not know how. I was a half-ghost Chinese Brummie, a make-believe phantom, a doppelgänger with a packet of Strawberry Chewits in her hand.

Audience

John A. Pitts

I've always had one. A make-believe one, I mean. A collection of people I bring together to form a sort of hyper-real panel of approval, an imaginary group to applaud and inspire every decision, perception and direction. 'What would they think if I did that? How would he behave in this situation? Would she be attracted to me if I acted like this?' I'm sure most people must have their own imaginary audience ... It helps us create a clearer reflection of who we want to be – where we see our position in the world.

But what happens when that reflection doesn't match up to the real person we stare at in the mirror each morning?

My name is John. I was born on a council estate in Sheffield, north England. My father was an African-American soul singer who came to Britain in the 1960s as a member of a soul group. My mother, a working-class white girl from Sheffield, fell in love with him when he was on tour and the rest is my history.

I grew up surrounded and nurtured by my white

family. It was my mother who raised me, while my father spent most of my youth working away from home. I was a minority at primary school in every capacity – one of maybe five 'coloured' children in the entire year. Most of my friends were white and, in order to avoid being deemed a 'Paki' (which would have been the worst thing possible at my age, in that space and time), my friends and I came up with a solid argument surrounding the fact that, though it was true I had brown skin, I was normal because my Mom was white. All the kids would bear witness to that when she picked me up at home time. I still had to argue against accusations of being adopted . . . but at least for the time being they didn't see me as a blackie or a Paki.

My best friend was Chris, a white boy with longish blond hair styled into 'curtains'- a look that I admired more than he'll ever know. Chris was a good friend to me. His family were quite well off compared to most of the others in the area and all the girls fancied him . . . Hanging around with a borderline Paki would have won him no brownie points. Hmmm, brownie points. I'm not sure why he befriended me, but I was grateful for our allegiance. Looking back, I suspect that he unintentionally and unconsciously recognized the fact that he was more intelligent, better-looking and more popular than I was in every aspect. I made a great sidekick. And, of course, I'd

never steal his thunder or stand a chance of going for
the lead role – people like me were never the lead. In
fact in most of my favourite films people like me
were the first ones to be killed off! Though never
articulated, I believe that there was always a silent
agreement between us about this fact, and we played
our roles well. But even with that subtle knowledge, I
managed to convince myself, and others, that I was
really just like him . . . white; the black bit was merely
an insignificant mistake, or a slight anomaly in my
pigmentation.

My Audience, Aged 8

- CHRIS: My best friend with the cool straight hair
  who all the girls had a crush on.
- EMMA: The white girl who was going out with
  Chris and who I, and most of the boys in my year,
  fancied.
- BROS: The famous pop duo who sported the
  fashionable ripped-jeans look.
- MOM: Who, in her all-encompassing, deeply loving
  way, might as well have been called God.

Then something happened.

As I began to mature through puberty I started
wanting to win. To be the lead role and the number

one, the hero and the guy all the girls wanted. So strong was my inferiority complex that I had to challenge it with arrogance. I became an awkward extrovert.

Around the same time I started to realize that my hair was never going to be straight like Chris's and people around me started to realize that I simply couldn't have been white. In fact, quite the opposite: society now saw me as a young black man and practically denied my association with the white race. My cover was blown in the winds of adolescence, but it no longer mattered, because I had found a new audience. An audience whose combined parts could be assembled to more accurately suit the image I saw every morning in the mirror, and the image the whole world seemed to be trying to tell me to fit in with.

I could be BLACK.

This was a revelation. Or perhaps, more in keeping with my ideas of black identity, a revolution! A whole new world of realization opened up to me. To be black was to be cool, strong, tough, stylish and anti-establishment. Images of rappers with baggy clothes, flashy hairstyles and expensive jewellery filtered through the various mediums of media a child was exposed to. And with my dad never being around, TV and music were the only things that really taught me how to be 'black'. Spike Lee, John Singleton and the Hughes brothers not only directed the colourful characters depicted in films such as *Do the Right Thing* and *Menace II Society*, but unknowingly directed my own self-identity, influencing my new choice of audience. African-American hip-hop artists like Public Enemy, Snoop Doggy Dogg and MC Hammer became my all-new demographic, and my every action would be tailored to suit their imaginary approval. The girls in my audience were still all white, though. A lifetime of training had ensured my brown eyes only recognized Caucasian feminine beauty. All my friends fancied white girls, so they had always been the biggest prize. And Chris, my best friend, was still around, although suddenly I was the one who had all the power!

I now didn't just look black but *became* black. Black was in my walk and my baggy clothes. Black filled up my vocabulary with slang terms like '187', 'beef' and 'nigga' – all words I hadn't fully grasped the meaning of. Or at least the historical or social meaning *behind* them.

My Audience, Aged 15

- NATHAN, JUNIOR, MARCUS, LESTER and a plethora of black youths who had a fearsome reputation in my area.

- 2PAC and BIGGIE: Two talented black musicians who died at the hands of gun violence aged twenty-five.
- O-DOG: The coolest character in the film *Menace II Society* who 'just didn't give a fuck'.
- EMMA: Chris's ex, who I was now seeing on the down-low.

Gyal started to take note too, you know. A nigga looked just like them rappers and badmen on TV. I grew some sick hairstyle with my hair in an Afro that all them bitches wanted to touch, and even got into trouble at school for 'dissing competitions' with my crew. 'Your mom's SO FAT . . .' I was from the ends too. You know the hood . . . where niggas was gettin' killed on a daily basis and peeps would listen to my street tales and look at me like the soldier I was. Them white gyal would marvel at me when I'd tell them all the gangstas I knew. 'Yeah, dat dealer is my uncle.' 'Yeah, my sis goes out wid this dealer.' 'Yeah, dat nigga wanted for murder is my next-door neighbour, man.'

Fuck being white . . . In fact the same moms I'd used as a tool to get respect was now an embarrassment to my big-man street credentials. The man dem were scared of was me, and I got nuff gash from gyal who thought I was a dangerous black kid. And in my head I was.

But then I got into sum beef at skool after I mash up some prick's face wid a hockey stick. Man was acting bad, so I had to show him a little suttin', ya get me? Dem pussy ole teachers cudn't tell me shit.

Then the phone call came, innit. For the first time ever . . . it was my pops cumin to pick me up from school . . .

Seeing my father's tall, dark frame striding behind the black metal railings and then into the school gates awakened a fear so deep I became a little boy again. All the posturing that had provided a forcefield to stop anyone knowing who I *really* was had disappeared. It was almost an epiphanic moment, one where I had to confront an uncompromisingly truthful emotion: FEAR. My father was never a violent man, or at least he wasn't around enough for me to truly witness much of his anger, but he had an aura and a look that could pierce my soul. When the headmaster told my dad what I had done, he looked at me with a strange mixture of anger and disgust. I broke down and started crying, begging for forgiveness. Right there, in front of my imaginary audience of rappers and gangsta-loving white girls, I fell apart, releasing my true colours, and I didn't care in the slightest. In fact, in the midst of my fear I felt almost free; all I cared about was the respect of a father and the embrace of my Mom.

It was a long, silent walk back from school with Dad that day, and the intensity seemed to be magnified by the strange silence of the early afternoon, experienced because of my temporary expulsion. When we got home I went straight upstairs to my bedroom and looked at myself in the mirror. Everything seemed more real than ever before ... more visceral. My big lips. My coffee-coloured skin. My soft curly hair. My chestnut-brown eyes framed by a cluster of freckles. And it was the first time I felt truly alone. Alone in a certain serenity. Like the calm feeling after you've puked your entire insides out, having digested something you shouldn't have, left with that bitter taste in your mouth. My audience of tough guys, rappers, girls, Chris and all those heroes of mine had left their chairs in my theatre of self. Either out of disgust at my performance or simply because the performance had ended.

And with the end of the performance, I began to stop acting. To stop allowing other people's needs and ideas of who I should be make me who I am. Whether they saw me as an 'almost white' boy who was 'allowed' into their club or, with this misguided perception, as a 'dangerous black man', I started to understand that the only audience I had to find in my life ...

... was myself.

My Audience Now, Aged 26

- JOHN: A TV presenter, writer, journalist and former youth worker for Sheffield Council. He likes long train journeys, playing football on a Sunday and crispy duck pancakes.

In the Middle of Nowhere*

Claire Frank

* 'In the Middle of Nowhere' is told from Claire Frank's daughter's point of view.

The plane is a nineteen-seater with two pilots who know everybody. Sometimes if that plane needs fixing, there's a seven-seater with only one pilot. I like the French one who says, 'Ça va?' to me so I can say, 'Ça va bien' back.

Usually the plane doesn't come on time and sometimes it doesn't come at all. Dad checks us in while we eat breakfast, because when it lands you can hear it from the house and then we know it's time to go to the airport. We have to hand in our boarding passes to the lady who teaches maths and we look through the shutters to see if anyone interesting is coming in off the plane. 'Look! Crystal wid she granny from Canada . . .'

The plane bumps up and down in the air so much that some of the ladies cross themselves and call out, 'Lord Jesus.' It makes my head ache and I get too hot, so I fan myself with the sick bag and grip the seat in front. Pastor Williams turns round and tells me, 'Sit still, child,' so I drop my head down quick. One day on the way back we saw whales with their babies in the sea below us and the pilot went round twice so we could get a good look. They *were right below us in the turquoise water, blowing up big spouts and thrashing their tails.*

I used to live in the Caribbean; I went to live there when I was three. The English adults used to say, 'Oooh, you are so lucky, all that sun and sea and tropical fruit. You're not missing anything here.' The English children used to say, 'Do you know Sean Paul?' Of course I don't know Sean Paul; I live in Barbuda. Sean Paul lives in Jamaica. Some of them people don't even know where the Caribbean is. Barbuda is small and quiet and nothin' much to do. It has seven churches, three shops, two bars, one restaurant, a school and a basketball court. If we need anything we have to go Antigua. 'You can't even get a ball of string in Barbuda,' Mum say.

So we go Antigua by plane – or the ferry, when it isn't too rough or out of service. It take fifteen minutes to fly and three hours to wait. It cost so much we never went much when we were younger, unless it was an emergency, like when my brother born, or our birthday, and then we go with Mum as a special treat, one at a time.

We'd hire a car with a stereo and air-con, an' go straight by the Guadeloupe pastry shop on the way into town and buy pain au chocolat and Mum real coffee. Then do the shopping – too-big-long-lasting-school shoes, Sellotape, a new cutlass, a bigger washing bowl. Then to the big supermarket to buy groceries, real cheese and yoghurt, and an argument with the supermarket gal to find the right kind of apple box with a lid to pack it all in. 'It's got to go on a *plane*,' Mum say, glaring at the bag packer and taking it out of the plastic bags. Then, if any money left, to Big Banana at the airport for a slice of pizza, wishing them hurry up, and listening for the flight, ready to cram it in your mouth and run to departures. Then when we get there they make us wait another hour, and Mum say, 'We really should walk with a pizza for the others.' But it always too late, and on the plane back to Barbuda there's a big fat somebody with a bucket of Kentucky Fried Chicken balanced on their knees and everyone else licking their lips.

Then I come to school in England for a while, so I soon get to know what England is like. It after Hurricane Luis, when the Barbuda school blew away. I hardly remember the hurricane, except Mum make we all get in the shower. It last for two days and one night. Granny was there on holiday, and she sing songs and play games with us till it was over. She make about a hundred cheese scones before the electricity went off and we eat them for the whole hurricane. We start to run out of drinking water but Mum say it will be OK; in an emergency we can drink the water out of the toilet, but the wind stopped just in time. When it end we went for a walk and had to climb over the electricity poles, but by then they had turned the current off. On the way Granny kiss the man who built our house because our roof stay on, and when we got down to the school our classroom was full of donkeys.

After three month of no school, Mum give up trying to teach us and we come to England to live in Granny's house. My brother get so excited about going to the seaside and when he first see it, it look so grey he cry. He learn quickly at school to support Arsenal and it's safer to keep your mouth shut, after he first see a dog on the street and think it was a pig it so fat, and make everyone laugh at him.

Mum soon get us into the same school as my white cousins. Everyone was rude to the teachers but no one got blows because it ain't allowed in England; the teachers *couldn't even look in your bag*. There weren't any other black children because we lived in Norfolk, which is still in the middle of nowhere. One boy come up to me and say he don't like black people, right to my face. I'm not even black, I said – I'm brown. Mum say nah bother with him because he come from a family where he been brought up like that. I didn't really mind, because my sister and brother are clearer than me, so some people think they are white kids anyway.

So we live with Granny in a village in the country-side, a bit like Barbuda but cold. The place is small, but in the town near her it was more busy and exciting. There are a whole lot of clothes shops, and a McDonald's and a cinema, and a double-decker bus that drive you there for £2, winding down country lanes in and out of every village, passing farms and fields of sugar beet. Then one day Mum chuck our things into the back of the car and leave in a huff and we get a flat over a restaurant where Mum work and we get all the leftovers. We get a bit tired of spare ribs and duck bones, but I get all ten of my GCSEs and learn to be a waitress and save enough money for a flight back home. And every now and then we have a funeral to go to and we go see Dad's family.

Those cousins live in Nottingham. Nottingham then seem like it so big, man. Full of cars, police sirens and people rushing about – but none of them lookin' at you. Every time Mum show us our old house and the hospital where me and my sister was born, and we always go in our old park if we have time and look at where we used to play. We buy plenty samosa to bring back to Norfolk from our friend's shop down the street and our cousin eat them all even though they live there all the time, and so we go back for more to eat in the car on the way back. And whenever Granny next get in our car she say, 'Claire, why does your car always smell of curry?'

When we go there the whole family want to see us and we visit all them house, one after the other. The last time I see some of them was in Barbuda; they always come when flights are cheap. Every few weeks a cousin or aunt or uncle come for a holiday and before long they want our jeep to go beach, but without paying for the gas. And these city people don't like country life much: they can't clean fish, they use up too much water having showers and one time Valerie even scream, '*STOP THE CAR!*' to get one fly out.

But after a while they get more used to it, and Mum and Dad have everyone over for a barbecue on the coal pot, and we have fried fish and Dad make rum punch and they bring plenty beer and we play loud music and talk all night until no more food or drink left. Sometimes in Nottingham, when all the family together, we start to feel like we back in the Caribbean, and soon we drink too much beer and soda and fill up with stew chicken and johnny cakes, and my auntie ask me, 'A when you a go back, Asha?'

I plan my holiday to go back for six weeks before I go to university and Mum let the others take two weeks off school. 'They can take me to court if they want,' she say, 'but it's important for you all to see your father. You're not just going to bloody Torremolinos,' and she pay for my brother and sister to go too and put it on another credit card.

Mum gives the three of us too many things to fit in the suitcase. Clothes for Dad, tools for the new house, food for the holidays and long letters attached to presents for her friends. This time when we get to Antigua I see the airport has changed. The lady selling fudge gone and in her place a whole lot more security than before. But I hear the music of King Progress shop playing the same tune as I have on my iPod and have time to buy a slice of pizza before the departure is called. We line up with fifteen others and old Pastor Williams beckon me over to his side – 'Come here, child. Carry this bag' – and shuffle out towards the Barbuda plane.

Eleven Years

Monika-Akila Richards

... men once slaughtered for a purer world,
trains riding six million into death ...

In a pretty, well-kept market town in southern
Germany, surrounded by fields and woody hills, my
grandparents live with two children. They inhabit
the top floor of a large three-storey house. The bay
window is shaped like a watch tower and over-
looks the train station and high street. In 1945, hidden
away in the attic, my grandfather, a civil servant,
builds his wireless. He listens to the BBC World
Service to hear the true state of play. At the same time
Oma (granny), a legal secretary, carries out her daily
shopping at the bakery and dairy farm. She steers
clear of the clean high street, lined with Third Reich
flags and the obligatory Hitler salutes. She detours
through the parallel Park Avenue, lined instead by tall
poplar trees and stone statues. She usually takes a
rest by the Germania statue, a strong-bodied woman
covered in moss. At the same time in the next town
live my great-grandparents, a policeman and cook

for aristocracy, hiding Jewish people in their house.

Close to the end of the war, my four-year-old mother is woken abruptly in the early-morning hours. She hears shouting and screaming. From the dark bedroom window she witnesses two uniformed men hauling away an old woman and man. They are thrown to the back of a jeep like two potato sacks. A woman clinging to her old parents screams and pleads. She is punched and gun-smacked to the ground. The order is given, the jeep doors slam shut and they drive off. Screams fill the night and my mother's mind. This desperate woman, Mrs Weinberg, is *Oma*'s best friend. Mrs Weinberg's daughter Tilly is mother's best childhood friend. The fact that they are not taken is always surrounded by rumours of intervention. Tilly dies of polio a few years later.

Four years after the war my grandfather dies of leukaemia, leaving behind my widowed grandmother, my eight-year-old mother and her five-year-old brother. Up to this day my mother often wears a little gold star with a Hebrew inscription. She says it makes her feel at home, says that her father had frizzy hair before he became ill. His sister, *Tante* (aunt) Anny, had thick jet-black long hair and high cheekbones. She says that our family stored unspoken secrets.

One secret did come out. At twenty my mother

fell in love with a Liberian student, Mr George Nyu
Johnson, my father. His features, stature and intensity of eyes were comparable to Sidney Poitier's.
In other words, he was drop-dead gorgeous. He was
charming and confident. He came from a wealthy
family with high political status. To be able to study
abroad as an African student meant you either had
influential connections or were able to pay your
way. For my father, both were true. On 16 August
1961 mother pushed me prematurely into this world.
Georgia is my middle name for the love of my father.
Her secret love and defiance were forever visible:
Rassenschande (race shame: a Nazi term).

The hospital misdiagnosed me with jaundice and
commenced treatment with red heat lamps. However, my yellow darkened into tan followed by
bronze. My features unfolded with button-black eyes,
full lips and stubby nose. The full head of jet-black
straight hair fell out and grew back frizzy as only an
Afro can. Nurse Maria fell in love with me and poured
out her heart, while my mother was not even trusted
to touch me. My father's charm went cold and took
on a political spin when he questioned my parentage. The Department for Child and Youth Welfare
took the matter to court. My mother had no choice.
My parentage was confirmed. I was told that my
father shook my mother's hand, as in a business deal,
congratulating her on the victory. The judgement

ordered him to make financial contributions towards my upbringing. Mother found a job in a children's home that would house her with me, but when she turned up on the doorstep with my rich colour in her arms, she was sent packing.

Monsters of the past had reshaped in busy reconstructions, shadows realigned to a new dawn after denazification. My mother's changed body and struck soul could no longer hold present and past trauma. She ran away to America. I was left behind.

Mutti von Brasselburg (Mum of Brasselburg) surrounded us with love. This rich middle-aged lady with gold-rimmed glasses and a heart of gold took in orphaned, abandoned, disabled and bastard children, and others, into her expansive mansion. *Mutti* poured her love like cake mix into a tin. Well contained, we were allowed to rise, and the healing aroma descended on us.

I fell in love with two blond twin boys, playing constant games of hide-and-seek.

I fell in love with the cool teenager in his wheelchair who smoked. I nearly coughed out my lungs when I took a secret drag from a discarded stub. He laughed till tears ran from his eyes, while tapping me on the back to ease my cough.

I fell in love with the bastard just like me, my dark prince, strong and bright-eyed with frizzy hair as only an Afro can be. His exuberance was breath-taking.

The outside world was full of strange shadows, suppressed monsters, hostile stares, finger-pointing and the overfriendly touchy-touchy of my hair and face that always left me feeling dirty. We, the loved children, protected each other with play and laughter. Every now and then the outside world would enter the mansion, with beady-eyed adults looking for children to take away.

I lost my twin lovers to a Swedish couple.

No one took my cool teenager or my prince.

No one took me. The big love in our hearts went unrecognized.

Tante Anny arranged the start of my schooling when I was seven years old. All *Mutti*'s children were deferred as backward, as a matter of policy. The customary starting school age was six. She placed me in a Catholic convent boarding school for girls. It was to provide me with a good education, discipline and, most of all, a religious humbleness. I kissed and big-hugged *Mutti* and left with a giggle, so sure was I of the forthcoming love.

> . . . *her breath shot upwards into the clouds,*
> *fixing her sight on the gliding plane.*
> *'One day, it will take me away. For this day I pray . . .'*

Elisabethenheim, the convent, is in a city called Würz-
burg. Its huge grey structure of thick walls made the
outside almost invisible and certainly inaudible. This
site housed several school classes and dormitories, an
industrial kitchen, a chapel, a laundry, a huge wash-
basin for our daily feet-cleansing ritual, bathrooms, a
gym/concert hall with a fixed stage, an old people's
home, the nuns' quarters and an infirmary. For a long
time we made contact with the outside world only on
our regular Sunday walks.

My dormitory held at least twenty-five kids in
white iron beds, white walls, white bedsheets and
pillows in the pitch black and some children's
sobbing. I had my first out-of-body experience as we
were taught to pray. So at bedtime, if rocking my
head from side to side did not blur me into sleep, I
made myself very still and prayed to Mother Mary
and my angel. One such night I felt a deep falling in
my belly, a rush in my head and there I was, floating
about.

This practice became my savoured ritual, which
was only possible when I was alone – in bed or in
the toilet. Being still and praying filled me with
utter peace. At school break times I stared twirling.
Holding out my arms, I would go faster and faster.
I blurred everything around me, looking into the
sky. Always the same nun gently placed her hand on
my shoulder and asked me to stop. Sooner or later

the twirling continued, until one day I tripped over my feet and cracked my ankle. So, with crutch and bandage, I sat still and faced the sky, looking for angels. Often silent white planes with outstretched wings flew past, leaving a white stream in the deep blue sky. That was good enough for me.

Eventually planes became what they were. I learned to keep quiet and observe the codes of the required behaviour. A particular look, a gesture, a raised voice or silence – they all had loaded meanings. I became the best-hidden secret to myself. I adapted like a chameleon, or so I thought.

Two girls became my best friends: Inge, with her sunshine smile and sad deep blue eyes, and Beate from Poland, with her long, shimmering chestnut hair. We often had fierce fights for top-dog status, but would defend each other if anyone dared to undermine our friendship. Oh, how I envied their smooth hair, that shine and beauty.

Having my hair cut was my terror. I would always be taken to the same hairdresser. Placed on a big red leather chair, large mirror in front, I shut my eyes tight and pretended to disappear. The hard clip of the scissors above my head shot like a missile down my spine, through my bottom into my right leg. It was impossible to sit still. The hairdresser was incapable of cutting my frizzy hair. Her despair or pretence that all was fine would often leave me half finished.

At worst I looked like a mad person who tore out clumps, leaving holes in my hair. No one could show me how to comb my hair either.

Wool stuck on to a brown doll. Early on, I ignored that strange growth on my head, did not touch it and made it my blind spot. In fact I blanked any mirror, avoiding the reflection of darkness emanating from me. I would pretend to disappear. I often had nose-bleeds and also had bed-wetting to contend with.

I remember that once an Indian girl with two jet-black plaits stayed with us. On our first meeting I liked her instantly. We beamed big smiles to each other and then stared on the floor. I wanted to pro-tect her. There was a delicate preciousness in her smallness and soft voice. Two months later she was gone. I was heartbroken. A long time later, another girl, bronze with high cheekbones and slanted eyes, appeared. As soon as we caught sight of each other's ashy, frizzy hair, her eyes flicked down and my head jerked sideways. We instantly recognized our shame. *Don't move, don't cry*, it screamed over and over in my head. I was holding my breath. My frozen self saw red drops tap the lino floor, like the beginning of a monsoon rain. Abruptly a hand pushed a white tissue against my nose, rushed me to the cool tiled bathroom and placed a wet towel on my head that calmed me down.

Love kept breaking through, like a sunbeam

through thick clouds. Every second and fourth Saturday *Oma*, my beloved granny, would bring me chocolate, biscuits and oranges. Sometimes she took me for *Kaffee und Kuchen* (coffee and cakes: a German tradition like have a cream tea in England) in a posh café. I felt all grown up drinking barley coffee and eating Black Forest gateau. The strangers' stares seemed less scary with *Oma* feeding me, laughing and joking, or taking walks with my hand in hers. All was perfect in these precious moments. I felt loved a thousandfold.

Tante Anny, a Red Cross nurse, worked hard and long hours in the big hospital. She visited me on the occasional evening. She also brought me fruit and sweets. Her cheekbones were still high, but her black hair was now grey and pulled back tight and straight. *Tante* Anny spent a considerable amount of what she earned on my upbringing. She was particular about the colour of dresses, blouses and skirts she bought me. She felt that my favourite colours, red and green, highlighted my brown skin too much. When I was older and allowed to visit her at the hospital, I'd have to go through the back entrance. For a long time no one there knew of me, or if they did they were not clear of my connection with this Red Cross nurse. I knew *Tante* deeply cared for me but could not deal with the shame.

Although I was a strong and healthy child I would

regularly fall ill. I know now that this was due to my intolerance of dairy, inherited from my father, and also to my increasing longing for my mother. Angelika, tall and lanky, became my compatriot in sickness. We often fell ill at the same time with earache and tonsillitis. If it was persistent, we'd be taken to Sister Bonifacia, the nurse under the roof. Sister Bonifacia wore everything in white, from her head cover to her shoes. Each morning and evening she would place freshly laundered light cotton towels over our heads, open the windows and make us breathe deeply. *Oma* would visit me with a net full of oranges. I would smell the cold air and snow on her coat and feel at ease looking at her face framed with her glasses. She sat next to my bed and passed me the peeled orange segments. Every act under the roof took on meaning: Sister Bonifacia's healing hands, our daily breathing exercises, *Oma*'s visits and the stillness in between. Under the roof a different prayer came to me, the one where you sit still and gaze into the sky and let the snowflakes blur your vision. The prayer was turned upside down. I no longer asked for my mother's return. I came to be asked. In the quietest moments I could hear my angel. Healing arrived and we adjusted to being back downstairs, mixing with our friends. The experience stayed with me.

As a group of girls we'd often play *Wer hat Angst*

vor dem Schwarzen Mann? (Who is afraid of the black man?) *'Niemand!'* (Nobody!) was shouted back. *'Und wenn er aber kommt?'* (But if he comes to get you?) was the response. *'Dann rennen wir davon!'* (Then we run away!) was screamed, then one girl would chase all the others and touch them 'out' until no one was left. Guess who played the frightening black man, chasing all the girls? I loved it, because I felt powerful and strong.

A selected group of us performed in a choir to parents and guardians or in the internal chapel. The music sister was cruel. She often reduced us to tears in the one-to-one lessons. She would hit us on our heads or press her fingernails to our temples and force us to continue playing the instrument while choking on tears and fears. Her overbearing presence always bore the threat of menace or unpredictable outbursts. One day she took me aside and stopped me singing in the choir: 'Well, I'm not sure what happened to your voice. It's the wrong sound really, too strong for this choir. It just stands out too much. You know what I mean. Too, too ... that's right, too niggerish!' She inspected my face for signs of distress, but to stay expressionless was my act of defiance. I hid my devastation. Music and song were my joy and adoration. *Well, then,* I thought, *I will sing to myself.* I stopped attending my music and singing lessons, providing no explanation. I started singing out loud in the particular long corridor that echoed my niggerish voice, knowing full well who was behind the closed door.

At the age of nine I became part of a new group: girls with special problems. The bed-wetting still continued. Our living quarters were the first ones to be modernized, with smaller bedrooms, a living and study area with a television and a kitchen. Sister Pia, the gentle hand on my shoulder, took charge of our group. She had acquired specialist training.

We often exchanged stories of our imagined family. I would point to passing planes and say that my father was sitting in there. 'So how does your daddy look, then?' Inge asked. 'Oh, he is really kind,' I replied. 'He has big eyes like me and grey frizzy hair. He, he ... wears gold-rimmed glasses and does important business. He wears a suit and has a very deep voice. He, he ... promised that one day he will come for me.'

I imagined how his family would surround me, clap and dance at my homecoming, while I would sing at the top of my voice in gratitude. My father surely loved me. He just could not get to me through these stone walls. On other days, my imagination made me see my mother waving from the plane window, with long blonde hair, kind smile and deep blue eyes.

. . . step out bright, on the pavement alight and stop,
shimmering outlines sharpen
the lady across,
high platforms, yellow dashiki (African tunic), sunglasses.
It is her . . .

In 1972, on a hot August morning, three days before my eleventh birthday, I got the news. Sister Pia told me that my mother was waiting for me outside. She had returned from the Caribbean, Grenada. I could hardly contain my excitement and buttoned up my blouse all wrong. I wondered whether my mother would recognize me. Sister Pia allowed me to race downstairs against all regulations. She took my hand when she opened the heavy door and we stepped outside. A woman stood on the opposite pavement. Her skin was tanned almost like mine. She had an assured pose, unlike mine. I suddenly pulled away from the hand, ran across the street and hugged my mother tight for a long time, my reconnection. She would make everything all right now. She would read me good-night stories, tuck me into bed and hug me often.

'I would prefer if you call me by my name, Ursula. I am a woman and a feminist, more than just a mother. I'd rather be your friend.'

It hit me with a kind of numbness and inability to understand. My internal question tried to explain:

75

Is that why she went away, because I made her a mother?

Mother tore in like a tornado, capable of destroying people around her. Her way of speaking and her actions often held rage and sometimes cruelty. I overheard her arguing with *Oma* about why she had never taken me to her town. Did she have a problem with my skin colour? I felt deep shame for my mother's attack. Did she not know that *Oma* loved me? I heard her shout on the phone to *Tante* Anny that she would never agree to me being adopted by her because of her stupefying religious outlook: '... and my daughter is *not* your little Negro sinner! She does *not* need saving! Got that?' Pow! She almost punched the phone back on to the receiver. I was confused. Why was adoption mentioned? Was my mother not mine?

I learned how to dance to soul music and calypso. That's when we started to connect, discovered our sameness. Singing along with these songs not only made me realize a black voice's power but also made me happy. Often Mother would open the top buttons of my blouse. 'Stop being so uptight and start getting hip,' she would order. I felt exposed, not daring to rebutton in her presence. She would forbid it. Mother wanted to free me and I wanted to be safe.

Getting to know my mother was often difficult, but I decided that I would never let her go again. To keep her would mean to become the safe for all her pain.

I would be the love of her life. I did not know then how it would take me to the edge. Mother detected racism and anti-Semitism like a pro and would expose it uncompromisingly. Her intentions were to radicalize me with urgency, based on her living through the Civil Rights movement in America, to prepare me to cope with the outside world, able to hit back. In this mission she would not see my desperate need for a mother's love.

There were, however, many precious moments that changed my life. They were the start of my self-discovery. My mother would provide me with insights no one else could. One afternoon a few weeks later she questioned me over her cigarette and coffee.

'So how do you see yourself?'

'What do you mean?'

'Well, do you *like* how you look?'

'How do I look?'

'You mean you don't know?'

'Course I do.'

'So . . . how do you look?'

'Fine!'

'Fine? This table is *fine*.'

'OK, then!'

'That chair looks OK.'

'All right.'

'*All right* is like *OK* and *fine*.'

'I don't know what you mean, I'm sorry.'

There was a long silence.

'Come with me. I am going to show you someone beautiful.'

Mother led me to the full-length mirror in the bedroom. Instantly I hung my head down. I thought I was being mocked and felt deep shame. I stared at my red shiny shoes with the silver buckles. *How could my mother be so cruel?*

Mother's hands started creaming me from my legs up to my face. A sneak look from the outermost corners of my eyes reflected a shiny bronze skin. When her hands moved on to touch my hair I instinctively shut my eyes tight, tensed up and felt a shooting pain down my spine and leg.

'You see,' she stated. 'Your hair is like many black people's. See how strong and proud it is. You are black and beautiful. Your hair needs grease to make it shine and comb more easily.'

Her hands continued to create a cool squishy feeling on my scalp with a sharp menthol aroma. I felt rubbing and an unfamiliar sound that pulled and combed my hair upwards. No dreaded hard clang of scissors, no words of exasperation, no unfinished business.

'Open your eyes!'

I will never forget what I saw in those first few moments. My hair looked almost like a halo around my head and glittered like stars in the night. I stared, then investigated my shiny face and arms and suddenly broke out into giggles. There I stood with my first Afro, smiling, unable to tear my eyes away from the mirror.

'Didn't I tell you you would see someone beautiful?' she stated, then she showed me a wooden Afro comb with long, wide-gapped teeth. The handle had a carved fist. It became the first utensil in my beauty care.

Mother sat me down, showing me a book with brown shiny girls with big smiles and plaited hairstyles. They were in spirals and geometric patterns, crowns and loose plaits, close to the scalp, more on one side than the other, up and to the back and so many more. We studied the patterns and instructions and our quiet conversation filled me with love and a sense of being understood. It provided the basis of my discovery of my identity. I truly found out who I was when I left Germany on a one-way ticket flight.

Invisible Heritage

Bel Greenwood

Romania was like a grey flower, a land of perpetual winter. Even when the sun shone it felt cold, and in my memory it is a country full of dust and ice.

When I came back from Romania I was pregnant. The father was Romanian and he didn't love me. I was just a way out and he soon tired of his attempts to charm me. I try to block him out completely, but even now thoughts of him trigger fear. I put him behind a sinuous wall bigger than the Great Wall of China – one that rises to the moon and crosses half the planet.

I try to block him out, but I save little pieces of heritage, magazine articles and pictures, a book by Dervla Murphy on Transylvania, for when my child is older and wants to understand the invisible past that is part of her creation.

We are invisible. I have decided that the only safe thing to do is to take us out of history and stop all the paths that lead to us.

But I can't deny the beauty and the beginnings of my child completely. Most of the time, the Romanian in her is submerged. We can go months without even contemplating that there is anything other than Britishness in her blood, but then something will remind me that half of her physicality is from over there and I will say sometimes, *My child is half Romanian*, as if it gives her a mysterious aura of exotic and dark provenance. Though that is a conceit I should really give up.

Sometimes I wonder, if I had never told her or anyone else – kept her Eastern European origin secret – whether it would have any meaning at all. If she and others didn't know that she had a crossing of borders in the geography of her flesh, the fact of it would be robbed of all meaning. I imagine then that I would be finally liberated from a constant feeling of unease that one day I am going to have to let her explore this hidden world.

As it is, the part of her that lies submerged and silent can easily be forgotten. If she were simply British, she could just be herself, living life here in happy innocence, with no disturbing cultural claims on her consciousness and identity to haunt her as she grows older.

She could still revel in the riches of all cultures and all identities that are different from her own without disturbance or heartache or a sense of individuated legacy.

Would she be free or incomplete? Is there something in our psyche that flowers in a rich slipstream of a consciously shared culture? Is there something in her that will call out for fulfilment and recognition until it finds an echo on the other side of Europe?

All I ever wanted to do was to keep her safe.

Country Bumpkin

Sethina Adjarewa

The market is in full swing. Women's voices buzz over the noise. The smell of fresh bananas, salty fish and sweet tropical produce infuses the air. The colours dizzy my mind with extreme vibrancy and beauty. I clasp the hand of my aunt and am being pulled through throngs of people. Legs, fat and thin, obscure my view. We're here to buy; a quick stop before going home. The ground beneath my feet is muddy and wet. My flip-flops stick as I walk, slapping loudly on the soles of my feet as they are suctioned from the ground. For a moment, the world around me pauses. I turn and see my flip-flop disappear in a muddy puddle, lost behind busy folk with baskets of wares piled high above their heads. I am small in their tall and hectic world. I begin to cry.

This remains my earliest and only memory of a life I left behind. Leaving Ghana, aged three, I began my life in England with my mother, father and baby brother. From the markets of Accra we moved to the fields of Somerset. Aged thirteen, on a trip to Notting Hill Carnival, I was served sugar cane for what I thought was the first time; I was shocked to find the sensation and flavour immediately familiar. My memory had failed, but my senses had retained the sweet, perfumed flavour of the chewy and refreshing cane I had eaten as a child in a country I could barely remember. This defining moment shocked me. My past was always there, buried deep within the person I had become. For reasons complex and despite my Ghanaian heritage, I have never been back.

My mother grew up in Somerset. She'd gone to boarding school and then on to Cambridge to study biology and zoology. As a child, she'd drawn images of Africa and had longed to go. After university, she enrolled in the Voluntary Services Overseas and arrived in Ghana in the mid-1960s. There she met my father, a taxi driver and some-time actor. They married and, in 1970, I was born. I arrived in the world four weeks early, a small 4 lb 12 oz yet strong and requiring no special care. My jaundice was treated by laying me on a straw mat in our sunny garden, surrounded by shrubs laden with papayas and guavas. The story was that I was delivered by the son of Ghana's leader of independence, Dr Kwame Nkrumah. This was my personal connection with Africa's independence from colonial rule. Two years later my first brother was born.

During her time in Ghana, my mother learned to cook Ghanaian food and make cornrow braids and fully immersed herself in the culture. She sewed us exquisite clothes of local cloth and wore traditional Ghanaian headdresses. A world away from the vicar's daughter from rural Somerset. My father's family welcomed her with open arms and, like many others, our family was bound by the strong ties of the extended family. My mother worked as a teacher and I was raised by aunts and my dear grandmother Maggie. Soon it was decided that we were to leave Accra for a life in England.

In 1973 I arrived in Britain from the depths of deepest darkest Ghana (as the Somerset locals believed). My new country imagined I'd lived in mud huts, walked naked, run with elephants in the wild and spoken in Swahili (the only African language many could name). Our arrival in the village caused quite a stir. The local vicar's prodigal daughter had returned, bringing her new, rather unusual family with her. For some, my white mother was a source of disdain, a 'tut-tut' in the village, with her wild black kids and tall dark Afro husband with brightly coloured tie-dye clothes and loud drumming music. Helpful villagers descended upon us, bringing gifts of second-hand clothes, used teapots, plates and appliances. We were the latest show in town and, for many, the first black people they had ever seen. From that day, I always knew that I was different and always felt that I stood out. With my out-of-control wiry hair and my dry, brown skin, I longed to fit in. My mother was the most beautiful person I had seen, with her pale and delicate face, slim body and long, flowing brown hair. My father, too, I believed was the most handsome man in the world. He was tall, proud, stylish and very, very black. They were the epitome of the 1970s 'right-on' couple: artistic, intelligent and well travelled, with a zest for life and a defiance of the ordinary. There I was, their child, and to which world was I supposed to belong?

It was something that I gave little thought to playing in the fields, finding fragments of Roman pottery in newly ploughed ground or plucking daisies from the grass. I loved the country: our glistening stream floating with minuscule duckweed, the crooked wooden bridge crossing into the fields full of poppies and tall grass. I loved visiting my grand-parents, hiding behind rhubarb leaves with Grandpa, planting flowers in the garden and stealing sweet juicy raspberries from his netted bushes. My father worried about what would happen to us when he dropped us off at the village school. As it turned out, I was protected by a group of kids. They looked after me and I made my first friend. We played games at school and I went to her house for tea and marvelled at her ponies. My brother and I were like any other local children and we adapted to our new life with ease. Life was good. Until those moments when someone reminds you that you are a nigger and different from the others.

By 1975, my second brother was born and we moved to Glastonbury. As I grew older, I became more aware of my dark skin. I always thought that the saying, 'Sticks and stones may break my bones, but words will never hurt me,' was absurd. Try telling a child that nigger, darkie, Paki, Chinky, blackie, Sambo, chocolate, golliwog, jungle bunny are not hurtful. Try explaining to 'polite' people who call you 'coloured' in an apologetic whisper that this is not the right term. Try telling your schoolfriends that chanting the infamous Jim Davidson saying, 'OOOO-OOOKKAAAAAAAAAAY', in a fake Jamaican lilt, doesn't make you fit in or make you laugh. As a child our Ghanaian names were a source of deep childhood embarrassment. The class would erupt in fits of giggles as my middle name was called, while I crumbled inside. Why, oh why, couldn't my parents have given me a 'normal' name, I used to plead? Today my brothers and I have continued the tradition of naming our children with their Ghanaian names. We hope that they will one day be proud to say Yaa, Adwoa or Akua as a tribute to their ancestral heritage.

By now my life in Ghana was a forgotten past. We were British. We joined in the street parties in celebration of the Queen's Silver Jubilee and the wedding of Lady Diana Spencer and Prince Charles.

We made our own Union Jacks at school and I coloured them in with care and pride for patriotic display. These events were marred by our racist neighbours. My romanticized country idyll was also a place of great hurt and fear. We were told to 'go home' and get back to Africa. My brother was thrown in a bunch of stinging nettles wearing only his shorts. I watched helpless as the big boys dragged him away and laughed at him silently holding back tears of pain and humiliation. I froze in fear when their Alsatian dog was let loose at me, biting my knee and shredding my favourite party jeans. On our city visits, we were sources of amusement for our black urban acquaintances. Our hair was untamed, as there were no Afro hair-care products in rural Somerset. Our accents were misplaced, a blend of Queen's English and Somerset twang. Wearing the most fashionable clothes we could find from our country high street, we ventured to the city. We were country bumpkins in an alien world. We were neither here nor there. I had no idea of beauty and felt ugly in the country with my wide African nose, dry bushy hair and dark skin. But I also felt ugly in the city, surrounded by beautiful black women with glistening perms or straight, glossy hair. Growing up, we always remained a few of only a handful of black faces in our towns. Several years later my father moved to the city, my mother remarried a white man and my third brother was born. Then some assumed we three black children had been adopted by a kindly white family. But as a mixed-heritage family we siblings bonded as any family did, never once seeing our half-brother as only 'half' of us; we were all the same. We three older children never had boyfriends or girlfriends until our late teens. Who would dare to date the only black faces in town? My father had told me to remember that 'success is the best revenge'. From those days, I became driven and determined. Our childhood remained one of intriguing dichotomies: innocence and experience; joy and pain; black and white; rural and urban; and African and British. Yet, out of these contrary states, an identity was forged and a unique personal growth began.

As soon as I was old enough, I left the countryside for a life in the city. I sought out the biggest city I could find. Spending several years in Los Angeles, I found anonymity in a city where many others seek to be noticed. There, I could buy my Afro hair products, not get followed around in shops and find the diversity I so desired. My friends were white, black, Indian, Korean, Hawaiian, Japanese, Irish and Mexican. There, ironically, I met my white British husband. But I was always homesick for Britain. We wanted our children to grow up in Britain so we returned, duplicating the scenario my mother had enacted thirty years prior. This time, though, we have returned to a city where my children are one of many ethnic faces in their school.

I now look back on growing up, playing in the fields, living lives of simplicity and joy as blemished only by experiences of isolation and times of trouble. My story probably isn't all that different from those of the other ethnic minorities who grew up in rural Britain. It affects who we are today, how we developed and what we became. It is only now, in my late thirties, that I understand how my identity is defined. I have my core identities and a mish-mash of identities that change over time. I thrive on this variety and I long for this diversity of character. I am a mother. I am a British-African or African-American, depending where I live. I am black. I am mixed heritage. I am a medical student. I am any one of a million things, all of which make me.

Thank You, Victor

Fay Dickinson

Dear Victor

I should have thanked you thirty-five years ago, but better late than never.

In the early 1970s I was the only non-white child at our local comprehensive school. Having an English mother and a half-English, half-Asian father I felt English and knew that it was only my dark skin and Indian appearance that marked me out as different.

On a wall not far from our house, someone had splashed the words, 'Wogs go home' in cream paint. This phrase was sometimes chanted at me in the playground. 'Wog go home.' I was also called 'Paki' and 'Gyppo', while one child even slanted his eyes with his fingers and jabbered in what he took to be an imitation of Chinese.

Once, when the teacher was out of the classroom, one of the remedial boys began to draw something on the blackboard. Disastrous mixed-ability classes, such as this one, had resulted in teachers spending hours with the slower learners and leaving us brighter ones to read a book. You'll remember that, Victor, because you were one of the clever boys. You and I started life in the 'A' stream. I liked that better. There was less prejudice than in the later mixed-ability classes.

This particular mixed class was a Religious Studies lesson and the boy, Don, who was drawing on the blackboard, had just stopped scrapping with his friend over whether Jesus was shot or 'hung'! Don drew a lopsided picture of a house and wrote 'niger hose' underneath it. He meant it to say 'nigger's house', but due to his ignorance and poor spelling no one took any notice.

I felt sick with apprehension in case someone realized and started laughing at me. A 'chocolate flavour' label had been stuck on my desk and last week a boy had hit me in the face with a plimsoll bag and shouted 'Enoch', referring to Enoch Powell's 'Rivers of blood' speech, which the lad had obviously picked up from his parents.

My best friend, who suffered from eczema and had cruelly been called 'Elephant skin' because her arms were sometimes cracked, bleeding and rough, said she'd rather have her eczema than my skin colour. Her skin looked incredibly painful and she was my best friend, so that meant not being white really was a terrible thing. I'm ashamed to say that during this time I wished that my dainty, blonde-haired, blue-eyed mother had married someone of her own race.

Anyway, Victor, let me remind you of why I'm

writing to say 'thanks'. We had a lesson with a teacher we didn't normally have, the ironically named Mr Black. I can't even recall what the lesson was now, maybe the vague and trendy General Studies. Someone, I can't remember who, made a stupid comment about my family, saying that we carried spears and rummaged through dustbins looking for food.

A very shy child and lacking in confidence, I felt that I was going to cry. I waited for Mr Black to stop the laughter and the taunts, but he didn't. This man should never have been a teacher. He sniggered, looked at the class for approval, turned to me and said, 'Why don't you tell us about some of your family's rituals?'

The tears spilled to the edge of my eyes and I was about to rush out of the room when you spoke up loudly and clearly. You said, 'Fay's family doesn't have any rituals. She's English.'

Victor, the class hard boy who wrote IRA on his exercise books, never spoke to me, but he'd spoken up for me. I was so grateful to you for your bravery. You were risking the jeers of your mates ('You fancy the Paki'), but you stood up to the bigoted teacher and you saved me from the taunts. I don't suppose they stopped, but I became better at dealing with them. Soon after, my brother joined the school, as did a delightful black girl called Joy, who had to endure the indignity of being called 'Burnt sausage'.

Victor, I never forgot what you did for me, even though I didn't thank you at the time. I was too timid and I daren't provoke any chants from the others.

Thirty-five years later I'm glad that I have mixed blood. I love my tan skin, dark hair and Indian features. In 1984 I spent a month travelling around Europe and people often queried my nationality. Was I Spanish? French? Arabian? Egyptian? How I enjoyed being exotically enigmatic.

No longer the shy child, I'm completely at ease with my skin colour. More than that, I exult in my mixed heritage. I'm proud to be different and I'm glad that my mum married someone from India and that the Indian she married was my dad. He was clever, kind and witty. Plus as a child he'd had a mongoose for a pet. How many dads can say that! Sadly, my dad died three years ago. He too suffered years of verbal racial abuse. I didn't know until I was an adult that when he was a young man he used to put talc on his face to try to lighten his skin.

As for my own school experiences, Don I could forgive for his ignorance, but there were no excuses for Mr Black's behaviour. Now in our twenty-first-century multicultural society I pass teenagers in the street all the time and they never refer to my colour. From skin lightening to enlightenment? We can but hope.

Anyway, thanks again, Victor, for sticking up for

me all those years ago. It meant a lot to me then. It still does now and I'll never forget it.

Best wishes,
Fay

Long Flight Home

Kristyan Robinson

Long Flight Home

Kristen Roffman

I have a headache. And my fingers tingle. It is difficult to hold the pencil and write. The weight of the boys' heads, one on either of my shoulders, pinned me to my bed while we slept for I don't know how long, numbing my arms and hands. They are still deeply asleep. I woke up with the book across my chest – *Finn Family Moomintroll* – and listened to their sweet deep breathing, their chests rising and falling out of sync under my hands, the whistle of the younger's exhale. I excise myself from this arrhythmic squeeze box and replace the duvet tenderly. Their cheeks are flushed and sweaty and they sigh deeply. The elder grinds his teeth a moment, opens and closes his mouth like he's chewing something, then rolls and reaches for his brother and settles again once contact has been made.

They'll be out for a while. They didn't sleep a wink on the plane. Their little body clocks will be duped into believing it's 6.00 in the morning and that they should be asleep, when we are now back in UK time and it's late morning – 11.00. Probably a mistake to take the night flight from Toronto. I thought that if we flew out on the 21.55 they would settle shortly after boarding and just about gather a night's sleep, which would help them get back on track in London. But they didn't sleep or even settle. They cried at take-off, pleading with me to stop the plane and let them out so they could go back to see their cousins, then they played with their seats, raising and lowering tables, stretching and banging the feet at the end of their eight- and nine-year-old legs into the chair backs of the passengers in front of them. They watched both movies, squabbled, argued and fought loudly across me over everything from a bag of peanuts to whether or not it was now time to change seats (again) so the other could have the window. Somewhere mid-flight, before the second film and after a spell of turbulence, the eight-year-old, Kuda, threw up mostly into the sick bag and quite a lot over my shoes, his teddy bear and my carry-on. I was desperately fighting sleep and dealt with the whole flight – with them, my two sons – through droopy lids and between nods of my head, stealing meagre slivers of sleep. I felt stoned and edgy by the time we hit Gatwick.

The Thameslink comes (finally) to take us to West Hampstead and we eventually arrive home from the station in a local minicab that stinks of cigarette smoke. I run a bath and I plunge them in, one after the other, then have a quick swirl myself, just long enough to rinse off the smell of recirculated air. Seven and a half hours with 320 passengers breathing nervously, digesting cheesy pasta bake with oversteamed broccoli and then farting. The hot bath convinces us of a need now for sleep. Still they make demands – 'Read to us!' But I know this will finish them off – a bit of reading in the fresh sheets of home, in my bed. I don't think I even made it to the bottom of the page before hearing sleep's stupor in my own voice.

I am a single parent. I am a lone parent. I'm on my own with my children. I'm separated. Sometimes I wished I could say 'I'm a widow', since this would not implicate me in any way (unless of course I was a widow as a result of murdering their father – the thought of which, I admit, had occurred to me from time to time as a solution during our seven years together). The relationship did not work out. He lied and cheated and this drove me crazy and sometimes I did feel murderous rage. My inability to deal with the situation calmly and patiently was my part in the whole messy ending, as was my lack of self-worth. I felt I was not enough, that if I could only cook better, laugh longer, work harder, be sweeter, make love more (but God, this was hard after having two babies in fifteen months), then maybe things would be all right. I thought it was my fault somehow that he strayed, and strayed, and strayed.

Some people didn't expect our relationship to work – two cultures, mine Canadian and his Zimbabwean, meeting in the middle in London. I was determined. I believed I was able to transcend these notions, to go beyond culture or at least to create a new one. At first he said he loved me and would be true; in the end he told me it was in his culture for men to take more than one partner. He asserted this, his cultural right, with gusto and thrust. I felt isolated at home with babies. The truth is that I never felt I had much of a culture as a Canadian with British grandparents. I was standard WASP – white Anglo-Saxon Protestant. We didn't have a strong culture like the Shona people in Zimbabwe, with music and dancing and certain foods and a whole system of manners. I was attracted to the *idea* of culture and tried to ingest it, to swaddle myself in the ancient culture of the Shona people. I lost myself in it, wearing beads, letting my hair mat into dreadlocks, learning to speak the Shona language and to play traditional songs – those used to summon ancestral spirits – on the *mbira*. Yet I felt deeply hurt by my partner's lies. I had gone more than halfway to meet him in his culture, but I drew the line at polygyny.

I remember other long-haul flights I've taken – to Zimbabwe, on my own in 1993 and again with my firstborn, Shorai, when he was six weeks old in the spring of 1995. That was different – tiny Shorai slept in a cot at my feet for most of the flight or nursed in my lap while I dozed. I was met by a driver holding a cardboard sign, the letters of my partner's sur- name neatly printed in black paint. The driver had left the village to work in Harare and had agreed, through a complicated exchange of letters, to meet me and Shorai and drive us in his uncle's Emergency Taxi to the village where my partner's family lived. I took my new-born son to his father's family in rural Zimbabwe, on my own, rather than to my own family in Canada.

I greet the driver in Shona, '*Makadiiyiko,*' while clapping cupped hands, right on top of left, one on top of the other, as is the Shona custom. '*Makadiiyiko,*' he replies, and claps his hands, man-style, flat, with his fingers pointed forward. Our exchanges of greeting continue until my Shona runs out – How are you, the baby is well, thank you, his name is Shorai, his father is fine . . . Then I stop. And I feel shy and scared and raw and alone. The driver's name is Garikai. He looks at me. His hair is cut short and neat. His complexion is dark – I remember when my son's father's skin was as dark in the months when he first arrived in London, how there was deep purple in his complex- ion. This has faded now after a year under the droopy grey canopy of English skies.

Garikai smiles and as we walk out of the airport

he reaches for the baby – my son – bundled in the pale blue waffle blanket I bought at Mothercare with the voucher the girls in the office gave me when I went on maternity leave. We bow our heads as I pass the baby to him as is the custom. Technically they are brothers, not by birth, but because they have the same totem or *mutupo*, the eland. The largest and slowest of Africa's antelopes, known for the curiosity of the wasps who build their nests in its shaggy beard. They do not sting the host, but I was beginning to learn after twenty months with my Zimbabwean partner and six weeks as the mother to his son that there was a sting that came from getting too close to the eland. I still felt his hand across my face, the tiny bumps that erupted like a rash precisely where his hand had struck me the night before. I was nursing Shorai at the time and the blow made my nose bleed, all over this tiny perfect baby in the only new baby grow he had, a present from an old childhood friend, posted from Canada.

The West Hampstead police told me that they believed he would continue to hit me. They gave me leaflets to read, which I did while trying to rest in the hotel where I stayed that night. One of the leaflets said that a lot of domestic violence begins when the woman is pregnant. What rotten luck. Just when the relationship is sealed through the sharing in the creation of a child, the seeds for separation are sown.

Still, I didn't believe them. I believed we could make it work and stayed on for another six years.

The first black person I ever saw was a boy called Robin. Although exactly halfway between Toronto to the east and Detroit to the west across the border, London, Ontario, was hardly cosmopolitan in the 1960s. Robin lived around the corner from me. He was adopted by a white family who already had a son – a small blond boy called Noah. Robin and Noah were younger than me and we only spoke to say hello. That's it. I passed their house on my way home from school and saw Robin bouncing a tennis ball with a racquet.

'Hello, Robin.'

He turns his dark face to me and does not smile when he replies.

'Hello.'

I pass again on another day and see Noah and Robin sitting side by side on the concrete step that leads to their front door.

'Hello, boys.'

'Hello,' they reply.

They share a secret; I can see it in their eyes. A gentle, quiet secret. Their love, the open-minded, compassion of their parents – Noah's biological parents and Robin's adoptive ones – to take in the orphaned black boy.

I'd seen black actors on TV. I'd laughed at Flip Wilson every week, particularly when he was his alter ego 'Geraldine'. I'd loved Bill Cosby as a kid, his warm humour and gentle depiction of childhood. There were lots of black musicians we listened to, but though Motown was close my parents stopped going to Detroit after the riot of 1967. I knew black people through the news reports – violent, aggressive, poor, drug-addicted, living in crowded American housing projects, so different from my own street and city. I feared black people, sang and danced to their music, laughed at their jokes, idealized them in their many various media manifestations.

And then there was Robin, right around the corner from me. A boy of eight, bit of a pot belly, wearing a navy-blue acrylic turtleneck that was slightly too small for him (the sleeves didn't quite reach his wrists) and navy shorts, barefoot, bouncing a tennis ball up and down his driveway with an old tennis racquet. His hair was thick compressed curls cut close to his head. The 'V' of his thumb and forefinger where it wrapped around the grip of the racquet was pale pink. I wondered about his parents, assumed they were Jamaican and dead. Although Canada was proud of its 'multicultural tapestry', it was essentially limited to white European with a Jamaican population in Toronto. There was not one black person at my school.

*

I haven't seen Stella for a few years – not since the boys were born. Stella Chiweshe, amazing *mbira* player and the reason I went to Zimbabwe in the first place. It was from her that I first heard *mbira* music, when I moved to the UK in 1989. What a powerful effect it had on me during the workshop I attended in Cardiff before moving to London. I felt I had to be by her side the entire ten days, and I was. The music put me in a trance, pulled me and pulled me until I was knocked off balance, changing my plan to pursue acting work and arranging instead to fly to Zimbabwe to stay with Stella, to learn to play. I did. She taught me how to play *mbira*, took me to Highfields, where I chose a beautiful-sounding instrument from a robust maker with fingers so thick I wondered how on earth he could pluck the narrow metal keys, but he could, he definitely could. And each time anyone in Zimbabwe played this astounding instrument I was transported. The repeated cyclical melodies with cascading high notes, tumbling down, beautiful when another player joined in, playing the same song staggered a heartbeat behind. The rattle of the bottle tops and tiny shells, wired to the gourd in which the *mbira* sits for amplification, buzz in sympathy with the bass notes, keeping time.

Stella taught me too about Shona culture, how to clap hands to show respect, to ululate, to wear beads, to enter the house of the spirit medium on my knees

in honour of the ancestral spirits. She showed me
how to string beads and snort snuff. She taught me to
cook *sadza*, and how to eat it politely, with my right
hand, tugging a peak from the thick, hot porridge and
rolling it in my palm before pinching some of the
vegetable stew between the pat of *sadza* and my
thumb. I learned to love it, pumpkin or rape leaves
with peanut butter, though found the Shona taste
for salty meat too much for my palate. I stayed with
Stella and soaked up everything she taught me, especially the *mbira* songs. It was, I suppose, inevitable
that I should then fall in love with Chartwell, another
mbira player, who toured the UK and met with me
and the other two *mbira* players in London at the
time to teach us new tunes.

My youngest son Kuda tells me he is 'one-quarter
Canadian, one-quarter Zimbabwean and one-half
British'. I carefully and slowly explain to him (and yes
I do patronize him, believing that he simply does not
understand) that this is not correct, that technically he
is 50 per cent Canadian and 50 per cent Zimbabwean.
He looks me coldly in the eye and tells me I am
wrong: 'I was born in England, I go to a British school,
my friends are British, I know my way around
London and speak with an English accent – I am
50 per cent British.'

*

I hadn't seen my family in Canada for five years. It was the first time I'd brought the boys to my home town since they were three and four, the first time since separating from the boys' father. My mother and father had come, individually, to England to stay with us a few times over the years but my sisters and their families had not seen the boys for five years. We stayed with my mom in her apartment in London, Ontario. London has changed since I grew up there, since I left in 1989. The town sprawls, with strip malls grasping at the edges of the city limits so that where once there were horses grazing and silos standing there are now Swiss Chalet chicken restaurants, Pets Galore and Hobby & Craft stores glued together in what look like prefab malls imported from America. All these strip malls look identical and the boys kept saying, 'Hey, that's where we ate with Nana!' only it wasn't, it was another Swiss Chalet that looked exactly the same as the others which were everywhere that wasn't the old part of the city.

My mother stirs her coffee too many times and slightly too loudly, her tiny teaspoon ting-tinging as it hits the inside of the porcelain cup. The boys are unaware (as, no doubt, is she) that this is unusual, but I sit up at this signal of her anxiety. Shorai is at her dining-room table, happily eating Rice Krispies with brown sugar and bananas, his ear to the bowl to hear the song of the Snap, Crackle and Pop crew.

Kuda prepares his Eggo waffles, whispering the catchphrase from the advert that he saw on TV – 'Leggo my Eggo!' – while pouring Aunt Jemima maple-flavoured syrup into the tiny square caverns. It's the morning of our last day. We will pack, have one final play date with the boys' cousins and tidy up loose ends before taking the coach to Toronto airport to board the 21.55. My mother says what I guess she's wanted to say for the duration of our three-week visit:

'You know, Kristyan, these boys look so much like you, they could almost be your own children.'

And then, 'In Canada when children are adopted the biological parents are obliged to provide a complete medical history. Do you know the medical history of the boys?'

There is a pause, a suspended moment, the time it takes for a crack on a frozen river to extend beneath my feet to the shore. For a split second I am standing, and then I plummet, crashing through the thin slippery veneer into an icy reality. My mother, deep within her, cannot reconcile the fact that her grandchildren are brown, that one has an Afro which he picks out and shapes with pride, that the other's short shape-up caps what his father calls 'a typically African head', the crown of the cranium drawn back, extending beyond his ears. They both have their father's full mouth and his very white teeth, but I guess it is the eyes that trick my mother. They have my eyes, there's no doubt. She looks at them and sees me but can't work the other features into the equation. She cannot recognize, despite the evidence of them looking so like me, that they are my (and her) flesh and blood.

Is it her fear or her intolerance that blinds her? I have no doubt that she loves the boys. She enjoyed playing cards with them while we stayed in northern Ontario in the cottage and she praised them often enough for helping her when she needed the table cleared or a Coke from the fridge. She was impressed by how well they read and how articulate they are when she asks them about their school play and about singing with Camden Music at the Royal Albert Hall. It was at her house in London, Ontario, so very far away from the London that I now call home, that her prickly feelings begin. I think she is uncomfortable with their blackness, perhaps even embarrassed in the place where her friends are, where she appears in public with them in one of the malls. She makes her comments in front of the boys, who stop and look together at her, then at me, then at each other. But they know who they are. At least, they know that I am their mother, that they are not adopted.

Throughout the day my mother's revealing comments pop into my mind. How different this is from the warm welcome Shorai and I received in Zimbabwe when I took him to meet his father's family. We were simply taken in and immediately accepted as family. I was helped with chores that were unfamiliar to me, carrying half the amount of firewood or water that other young women carried. Shorai was passed around, held and loved by the entire village. They kept him from me for some time in each day so I could rest. Once I walked back from collecting maize grain that dried in the sun and saw Shorai away off in the distance, tied to an old auntie's back while she sat harvesting peanuts. There was joy at our arrival; there was no embarrassment or shame. I wonder why there is such a difference. I guess it is because when you don't have money for clothes and you pray for rain so you'll have food in the winter you don't worry so much about the appearance of things. If the baby's cheeks are round and he's alert and strong, it's less important if he's lighter or darker than the other babies in the village. In my home town, or at least in my family of origin, the appearance of things sadly counts for more.

But then, this is my fantasy. And it's too black and white. For I do not speak Shona well enough to know what is really being said, and nor do I know any of the villagers well enough to read the subtle nuance of their expressions, their response to our arrival. But what I see is this: that my actions send concentric circles out, affecting those close to me. In the wake of my own journey my mother struggles, at times splutters and sometimes chokes.

We board the plane and I stash our bags above our heads and below our feet. I take out the chocolate I bought for us to share. I look at my children, their eager faces lighting up. They are my sons. We are going home, back to London, England, where their schoolmates come from all corners of the globe, where our street is filled with rich and poor, black and white, and where our own friends love and accept us as we are. That is what home feels like now.

Torn

Rashid Adamson

Spring 1986, my dad, Mohamed, my cousin Khaliq and I were driving to Bradford. I was sat in the back and could almost taste the odours of Khaliq's Hi Karate, Dad's Old Spice and my Aramis that permeated the air of the blue Ford Cortina estate.

We were going to visit members of my dad's extended family. They would sometimes come to Middlesbrough, where my dad, our mam and my brothers and sister lived, but at least once a month my dad would travel to Bradford. As he was the elder of his clan in England, he would have to be consulted on all matters that affected the family dynamic.

His approval was required before most important decisions could be made. He would decide who was ready for marriage and whom they would marry. He would rule on business and financial matters, making sure money was filtered back to Pakistan, to support and strengthen family and buy up land and property. As well as this, he made sure that all family members were toeing the line and staying out of trouble.

Since I was a kid, I had been the one who

accompanied my dad when he went off on his visits. OK, it was difficult and often very boring going with Dad to see his relations in Bradford, London, Birmingham and wherever else our travels took us, but I put up with it to show allegiance to my dad's cause. In addition, I felt a sense of well-being, felt comfortable in my skin, when we went to Bradford.

However, now just short of seventeen, I had stopped going on these family visits as much as I did when I was younger, for the simple reason that the older I got the more I was told it was time I was getting married. And I was aware that I would be pressured today, pressured into being a dutiful son who should accept what was being spoken of more and more frequently. The arranged marriage was beginning to leave the talking stage and progress to the arranging. My dad had already told me he had spoken with the 'owners' – well, he said 'parents' – of females who may well be suitable for me.

He said I could choose from hundreds of eligible women and have a house with my new bride as a wedding present. I could also still live the life of a single man, send her to Pakistan, for months or years, as I required. 'Nothing will really change,' he said. 'You can still have girlfriends. You just have to be careful and keep things quiet.' I was tempted to buy into the package of riches, property, hedonism and malleable religion that was on offer, even though it didn't feel right, and I knew I would be marrying, primarily, to please him.

When he preached to me about doing things 'properly' and having an arranged marriage, I wanted to say, 'Why didn't you?' But I knew the response would have been a good hiding, for our mam, who was always to blame for her kids' disobedience, and for me. He would also get on his high horse and give me a sermon on how stupid he was and what a mistake he had made by not having a Pakistani wife and proper, obedient children (which in reality, I would find out at a later date, he secretly did have, tucked away in Pakistan).

I sat in the back of the car and felt isolated and alone as my dad and Khaliq talked in Urdu. I was sixteen and caught in the headlights of life. The last thing I wanted was to get married. I wanted to 'live'. I knew it was traditional for Pakistani kids to have an arranged marriage when they came of age, but my problem was I did not consider myself a Pakistani kid. I was the son and heir of a mixed-up, mixed-race relationship that had birthed a sister, Yasmin, a brother, Hussain, and me. My English mam had two more sons, Gary and Brian, from a previous marriage, but the clash of personalities and cultures meant both had left home at sixteen and seventeen.

Growing up, I was always caught between two worlds, two faiths and two cultures. We all grew up tolerating, putting up with my dad. He was a dictator who had been bearable in the past (through necessity), but now we kids had reached an age that was suitable for marriage there was no way our mam could stand aside and let him dictate on this issue.

A year earlier, my dad had begun to start arranging a suitable suitor for my sister. He even brought him over from Pakistan, a cousin who was supposed to marry Yasmin and thus obtain a visa to live in England, the land of opportunity and free enterprise. This was when our mam took the bold step of standing up to him and saying that it was up to us who we chose to marry and when.

My dad did not like this insubordination, but he knew our mam would no longer lie down and accept what he said as gospel. She had put up with his dictating for almost twenty years. Now we kids were older, she began showing signs of resistance.

For as long as I could remember their relationship had been a loveless one, fuelled by contempt. He had grown to despise Western culture and values and he had taught her to despise him and his perverse religion. Looking back, I don't think they ever knew love. I believe they opted for convenience rather than love.

Anyway, to return to the blue Cortina. As I looked at my dad from the back seat, I could see a Pakistani man who had attempted, but failed, to leave the fold and assimilate into a Western lifestyle. Most people knew him by the name Eddie, because it was more convenient for English folk than Mohamed. Around them he would laugh and portray himself as a man who was easy to get on with, very friendly, but in reality he despised English culture, which he believed was pale and insignificant beside his own culture.

He would often bring the *maulvi* (his priest) to our house to cleanse us kids by laying his hands on our heads and praying for the evil spirit to leave us. We knew that what he considered as evil spirits, we considered Western traditions and values. To him music was evil, drinking was evil, smoking was evil, not speaking Urdu was evil, having English friends was evil, not praying five times a day was evil, having a girlfriend was evil, not fasting was evil, acting English was evil . . .

Dad tried relentlessly to make us into Pakistani kids. Every time we visited friends and family, I would become the topic of conversation. Does he speak Urdu? Does he say his prayers? Does he fast? Is he getting married?

They knew the answer to these questions was a big fat fucking 'NO' but they'd ask anyway. I felt like they were doing it on purpose to get at my dad for not raising his children in the proper fashion. From childhood, I had sympathized with my father's dilemma. He could not be the English father I wished

I had, just as I could not be the doting Pakistani son he wished he had. I respected him for being true to his beliefs. I was, however, confused as to why he had not remained true to those beliefs when it came to his own marriage.

If I had been brought up by parents who were both Pakistani, I may well have freely accepted an arranged marriage. However, I hadn't. I had been exposed to the intrinsic values of two cultures and I favoured those of the country I lived in.

Strangely, I did think I had a duty to obey him and to make him happy. I did love him; moreover, I didn't want to hurt him, because I had realized at an early age that most Pakistani lives were played out in a community arena and saving face in that community was of the utmost importance.

It was obvious to me that he saw me as his only hope of showing his community that he had not failed totally in his Islamic duty. I had been groomed for his purpose from the start. I was always number-one son; he obviously favoured me, as my temperament was most vulnerable to his persuasions. Therefore, my vulnerability left me open and defenceless against his constant attack on my conscience. My siblings had chosen to adopt and adapt solely to the English half of their heritage, but although I wanted to adopt that heritage also, I felt that if I did so I would be losing part of myself. But if I did the right thing by my dad, I would be disappointing the rest of the family, especially our mam, not to mention the huge gamble I would be taking with my own future happiness. As much as I wanted to make my dad proud of me, I was very doubtful that I could go through with it.

I told myself that when we got to Bradford I would speak to my uncle Talib. He was not like my dad; he was a good bit younger. He had an arranged life, but he was a little more tolerant and he understood that we were not traditional Pakistani kids. I hoped he would advise me, maybe even talk to my dad and make him understand that an arranged marriage was not a good idea.

Uncle Talib had settled with his family in Bradford to be closer to the large extended family. Before settling in Bradford he had lived with us for some time in Middlesbrough. He worked as a shipbuilder. I remember how he acted as a mediator then, when we kids were in trouble. He would always be on our side and speak of the virtues of prudence to our dad, saving us from many a good hiding.

It was about 11.00 in the morning when we arrived at Uncle Talib's house in Bradford. It was a typical Yorkshire stone terrace, sand-coloured and scarred with soot and grime. Walking in, it was immediately apparent that something was wrong.

Uncle Talib and two of my cousins, Khadim and Mamood, were in the front room. Mamood was wearing his bus driver's uniform. Talib was pacing up and down – the other two men were seated on the sofa, leaning forward with their elbows on their knees. They were surprised when we walked through the door. My dad did not always inform people that he was coming to visit.

I had never seen my uncle Talib like this before. He was raging like someone possessed. He was a handsome man who was always smartly dressed, never without a shirt and tie. Today he was ugly and unkempt. His normally clean-shaven face was stubbled with more than two days' growth. It was the first time I had seen him appear mean.

Looking at Khadim, I noticed the scar that sat above his right eye. I remembered then how he had got it, six or seven years earlier, when he was about eighteen. My dad and Talib beat him with sticks, bats and fists because he had been seeing an English girl.

My dad, Khaliq, Talib, Mamood and Khadim began a heated conversation in Urdu which I couldn't fully understand, but I did know that whatever was going on was serious. After about twenty minutes of frenzied debate, Talib went upstairs. He came down holding a canvas bag with what appeared to be a baseball bat and metal bars poking out from the top. Khadim and Mamood stood up and the three of them made towards the front door. I stood up as if to go with them, but, as they left, Talib snapped and told me I couldn't go.

Talib's wife was in the kitchen on her own. I gathered the children would be at school. She and Talib had twin boys about five years old and a daughter who was a year or so younger. I was looking forward to seeing the twins and their sister; I hadn't seen them for over a year. They were a real handful and very spoilt, but very funny and cute.

Uncle Talib's wife offered us some food, but I had already talked my dad into going to the restaurant we usually visited when in Bradford. We had planned to go there and then visit Sulaiman – my dad's sister's husband – later in the afternoon. And so, still wondering where Uncle Talib had gone, I went with my dad and Khaliq to the Sweet Centre on Lumb Lane in Manningham, where the food was as delicious as ever.

It was 1.30 when we left the restaurant to go to Sulaiman's house. I hated going there. I didn't like him and he made it clear he felt the same about me. To be honest, though, I think he just didn't like the fact that my dad was with a white woman and had half-breed kids.

Sulaiman's house was a frenzy of activity when we arrived and I could not understand what was being said. Talib's wife, who had heard that something had happened, was in the kitchen, crying, as were several other women. I stayed in the hallway while my dad and Khaliq went into the front room, where Sulaiman was sitting talking to three men I had never seen before. The men shouted for about five minutes, then we left.

I asked my dad what was going on when we were back in the car. He told me to be quiet and said, '*Bismillah hir-rahmaan nir-raheem*' (In the name of Allah, the Most Gracious, the Ever Merciful), as he always did when he started the car or before he ate. He said it, pretty much, before he did anything. Then he and Khaliq began speaking loudly in a manner that seemed very agitated and disturbed.

We drove to a part of Bradford I had never been to before. We approached a street and I noticed a police roadblock at the end of it. We drove straight by it and my dad and Khaliq began to speak in an even more ferocious tone. I made out the Urdu word for dead but had no idea what was going on.

A quarter of an hour later we were driving towards home. We travelled in silence for about forty minutes, then stopped at a red telephone box on a country lane, just before the approach to a small Yorkshire village. After making a call my dad got back in the car and spoke to Khaliq, once more saying '*murihage*', the Urdu word for dead.

'What's happened? Who is dead?' I asked repeatedly, knowing I didn't want to know.

'I don't know,' said my dad eventually, in a very angry tone.

Then he told me that Talib, Khadim and Mamood had gone to sort out a disagreement with some people and all he knew, at this time, was that one of them had been killed.

The car was silent all the way home, but my mind was deafeningly busy, convincing me Talib was still alive. At the same time my head was out of the window, throwing up the food I had been eating while the murder took place.

From the back seat I looked at my father with disgust. I felt nothing but contempt for him and all he stood for. The empathy I had with his plight had vanished. I wished that it was him who was dead. He, who created children and brought them up to believe the society they lived in was evil and that only by following and believing in him would they know happiness.

I hated him for not being the same as other kids' fathers and for being a dictator who would speak without listening. I wanted a father I could talk to, maybe have a pint with, share a laugh and a joke, see a football match or watch a movie. Although, before, I had been aware we would never do any of these things together, I had thought I was 'cool' with that. However, as we drove back to Middlesbrough I began to realize I was far from 'cool' with it.

We arrived home about 6.00. I walked through to the kitchen, where my mam was cooking.

'You're back early,' she said.

I said nothing; I waited to see what my dad had to say.

Taking change from his pocket, he told me to go to the shop and buy cans of Coke and Fanta. I opened the fridge to see it stocked with a variety of canned drinks, but I said nothing and left.

When I got back ten minutes later he had gone. Mam said he had returned to Bradford. She then started quizzing me about what had happened. I told her what I knew and asked her if she knew any more. She said she didn't. I believed her.

It was about 8.00 or 9.00 that evening, 30 April 1986, when the telephone rang and my dad told our mam, 'Talib is dead.' He never went into any of the details. He just said he would explain when he got back in a couple of days.

When he came home two days later he brought cuttings from the *Yorkshire Post*. According to the newspaper report, three men had pulled up outside a house on Fifth Avenue, Bradford. A running battle had ensued; iron bars, knives, an axe and a garden fork were used as weapons. Talib Hussain had died soon after the fighting ended. He had deep stab wounds in the chest and back, a fractured skull and was left with a garden fork stuck in his stomach.

The violence, the newspaper said, had followed a series of minor skirmishes in Bradford a few days earlier. It was thought that the dispute was over a piece of land in a village in Pakistan. Hukham Dad, Sobat Khan and Khalid Hussain were members of one group and the opposing faction consisted of Talib Hussain, Khadim Hussain and Sultan Mamood.

That day, and over the coming weeks, I started to realize that I had to remove myself from the barbaric and controlling clutches of my father's backward culture. By leaving it behind I would not be losing part of myself, as I had previously thought. Instead there was a chance that maybe, just maybe, I would become whole.

Head battered, confused and bemused, strangely I felt enlightened and empowered. This is what I have been waiting for, I thought. This is the perfect opportunity to go my own way. I thought, fuck him and his stupid fucking culture, and fuck Islam. He, his culture and his religion had been the bane of my life. If I fucked up because I hadn't listened to his advice, so be it. I could no longer martyr my life for his cause.

For the first time in my life I felt free from his spell and decided to make a life-affirming decision. Whatever the consequence, I would no longer be a snake to my father's charming.

I spoke to our mam and told her that I felt like I

was being pulled in opposite directions, that she had my left side and he my right arm and leg, and both were pulling me into their own dimension. I knew that both truly believed they were doing what was best for me. Unfortunately, the result of their actions left me feeling alone and guilty. I felt guilty because I could not please them both.

I told our mam that Talib's death had opened my eyes and made me see things a lot more clearly. I told her that I felt like a prisoner captured and chained by my father and forced to comply with his demands for the sake of duty: a duty that I had bought into as a child for the sake of gaining his approval and respect.

'I know things have been difficult lately,' she said. 'And now you kids are older things will not get easier. Your father's like a man possessed with this arranged marriage palaver and he won't let go of it. I haven't told you yet, I was waiting for the right time, but I've managed to get a mortgage. Gary and Brian helped me and I've put in an offer for a house. Everything should be sorted in about four or five weeks. I'm leaving him.'

I was shocked and dismayed for a moment, not because of her announcement, but because it was clear that I was the only one, apart from my dad of course, to be left out of the loop.

'How come you haven't told me before now? Did

you think I would have spilt the beans? When were you going to tell me?'

The questions were angry, but inside I felt conflicting emotions. Part of me was overjoyed and yet, at the same time, part of me was saddened to think of my dad abandoned and alone for nothing more than being true to his cultural and religious traditions.

'Maybe, I should have told you before now. I just felt it would be easier for you with less time to think about it. You think too much and I didn't want you worrying unnecessarily. I know how difficult it will be for you to choose whether you come with us or stay loyal to your father. I've tried not to interfere, but either way you know fine well that we cannot go on living like this.'

I looked across at our mam sitting in the chair in what had been our front room for the last four years. I thought about how she had martyred her life for us kids and after twenty years of suffering, mainly for our sakes, she was entitled to redemption. I watched her light a cigarette, take a deep drag and hold it longer than she usually did. Eventually she exhaled and the smoke floated between us.

'You are a special person, son,' she said.

My emotions were in chaos.

'You always see the best in people regardless of the situation. Look at your brother and sister and Gary and Brian – they feel nothing but hatred and anger for your father. You're different. You don't know hate. You see things from a much deeper perspective. You understand that your father is doing what he believes is for the best. Whatever you decide, remember I love you very much.'

It was several weeks later that the police released Talib's body. My dad took it back to Pakistan and was gone for four weeks. In that time the keys to our mam's new life came through. She did a moonlight flit in the daytime, along with my brother and sister. Together they moved into their new life. I went with them.

Ten Acres and a Truck

Sophia Al-Maria

My grandfather Amer Jaber Al-Dahabeb Al-Murrah died in the locked cab of a flaming pickup truck. Great-uncle Shakhbut and his two youngest children died in a rollover. The smallest, aged four, was steering on his lap. Matar and Hamad were trapped in the cab of a 4x4 during a sandstorm; a dune shifted as they slept and the two men were buried there for months before they were found. Little Afrah Abdul Ali was backed over by her grandfather while building a sandcastle behind the tyres of his truck. Khaled, Ali and Dheeb were crushed by an airborne car while watching a drag race in Dammam. Aunt Moza was thrown from a moving Oldsmobile while seven months pregnant by her husband, Saeed. The thirteenth child of my uncle Musa was missing for half a day before they found the infant in the back seat of their broiling car, suffocated.

Suffice it to say, my family's relationship to the automobile is a fraught one.

In the late summer of 1982, not long before I was born, my mother's golden Scirocco with thin rosettes and a Pegasus decaled on the hatch of the hatchback was pummelled in a hail of gunfire. When asked, mother had always flatly answered, 'It was sprayed up by a drink driver.' Of course I never believed her. But years later, when the Scirocco was sent out to pasture, wheelless, stripped and permanently suspended on stilts in a neighbour's overgrown backyard, I asked, 'No, but seriously, Mom. About those holes . . .'

Father was bright-eyed and bushy-moustached when he landed in California in 1978 with a Saudi scholarship and big aspirations of becoming a long-haul trucker. In my favourite photograph of the early years he is decked out in aviator specs and a stiff white trucker cap with OPEC stamped on the front. The Polaroid frames my swarthy dad against a velvet curtain the same colour as his skin. The main focal point becomes his wide, bright grin topped with a handlebar moustache. He is giving a strained thumbs-up between two larger-than-life wax statues of Kenny Rogers and Willie Nelson.

On his quest for the open road, my just-off-the-boat father went quickly through a series of cars: in San Diego a Silica, in Portland a red Chevy pickup, in Tacoma a Grand Prix and a Subaru in Helena. It was there in Montana where he decided to become a rodeo man instead of a roughback trucker. It was also at the rodeo where he met my mother, a blonde berry farmer's daughter from the Puyallup valley. Father had just sold his Subaru Brat to a hick who'd knocked out its windows and used it for the demolition derby and had spent his entire Saudi stipend on bailing a drunk and disorderly friend out of jail. For the first time he was truly immobile, an uneasy state for a Bedouin man. He was vulnerable and stuck, and then my mother came along.

She saw my father from the stands being harangued by a grizzled old woman: 'Hunny, yer too short an' swarthy to be wearin' that white cowboy's hat!'

Mother trotted down the hot bleachers and saved my beleaguered father from a round as Arab rodeo clown, snapping back at the hag, 'Good guys wear white hats and ride white horses, lady!'

So it was that Mother and Father drove, hands interlocked on the gearshift, through Idaho and the Scablands, over the Snake river and into the foothills of the Rockies. The mysterious holes in the golden Scirocco were in fact a memento of my parents' first ride together.

The way Father tells it, a drunken man in an Oldsmobile went weaving over Chinook Pass and was careening near the edge of a cliff when he honked his horn. The drunk man shouted expletives back. Mother rebutted with characteristic charm and flashed a few vulgar hand gestures. Two flashes of light hit the rear-view, they felt the bullets hit the car. *Then* heard the sound of the handgun in close succession.

Near-death experiences and velocity tend to change time around a moving vehicle. In seconds the summery swell of their all-American love story was tainted by gun smoke and singed leather.

A decade later Father still hadn't obtained a big-rig or tamed a bronco. Disgruntled and homesick, he returned to the Arabian Gulf to seek better fortunes in the boomtown that his region had become. He told Mother he missed hearing the mosque's *athan* (call to prayer) on the radio and left. He obtained a job on an oil rig off the coast of the United Arab Emirates, where he was stranded for two months at a time. He's long since given up on ever affording an eighteen-wheeler of his own, but he still keeps his cassette of 'On the Road Again' in the glove compartment half-melted beside his Qur'an tapes. Left behind with two mutt daughters in the rubble of her young husband's broken American dream, Mother moved us to Grandmother's homestead: a raspberry farm on the banks of the Puyallup river. Securely situated on the cul-de-sac of a dead-end road, Mother set about building the first of what would be many new lives constructed around our absent father. She got us on to food stamps, started car-pooling to night college and stopped wearing her hijab. It was a hopeful time, with no men and no vehicles in it.

*

Our tribe, Al-Murrah, was far from any city or town when the first automobile was received in Qatar. They say the single-cylinder, eight-horsepower Rover was a gift from the Queen of England to the Emir, Mohamed bin Thani. The miraculous vehicle was driven to the palace by three British military men. The walls of the palace were very tall and embedded with wooden spikes. The three British emissaries had waxed their moustaches for the occasion. Great studded gates were opened and the dapper auto puttered over the threshold. The silver grin and wide gills of the thing were menacing to those present and the welcoming party shrank back when the British men rode across the courtyard inside the body of the shiny beast.

The Emir was pleased.

He drove a few doughnuts in the courtyard and then invited the red-faced men into the *majlis* (men's sitting room) for tea. The men laughed jovially with one another as a black sea of misunderstanding began to bubble beneath them and the Rover waited patiently outside. It seems that the Emir did not have the foresight to see it as a harbinger of great riches. The Al-Thanis, though royal, were never thought to be a very visionary family. He ordered another for the crown prince and moved on to the subject of horse racing. In the evening, when camels were brought to escort the three men back to their quarters, they found a tray of roasted lamb and a basin full of water had been laid out before the grinning grille of the car. The cold meat and still water had been left untouched.

The first automobile belonging to my grandfather Amer Al-Murrah was a sort of 'ten-acres-and-a-mule' compensation from the government in the form of a white pickup truck without a make, logo or brand. He preened his truck with the same meticulous and gentle touch with which he tended his white she-camel. He decorated the dashboard with her colourful feed sack and muzzle and constantly monitored the truck's innards even though they were the simplest form of internal combustion. The thing was outmoded long before the family received it as recompense for being displaced by the oilfields in 1970. Although my grandfather was adept in the ways of the land, he had to learn to drive from his teenage son.

A few years before the truck came to the clan, Uncle Ali had learned to drive from an oil truck driver. He had waited beside the only nearby road which ran from the oil field to the main highway. He was being sent to the city to get medicine for his mother's 'sugar' disorder. At dusk he flagged down a truck that was hauling a huge silver tank. This driver took him to the city and taught him how to drive the twenty-five-ton diesel truck. My then twelve-year-old uncle steered and changed gears from the truck driver's lap while the man pumped the gas.

The family's new pickup had a deep bed and large treads on wide wheels. Their camelhair tent was pitched in the back of the truck. Those who couldn't squeeze into the front, piled into the back under the roof of the makeshift mobile home. The best spot to sit was huddled behind the cab of the truck, where one was shielded from the current of hot wind running through the tent's weave. Camelhair tents were equipped for almost anything but being stretched on to the back of a truck and hurtling at seventy miles an hour down a sandbank.

When my grandfather ceased to travel by foot (human or hoof) and opted for the horsepowered wheel it was a great loss for the Saudi police force. Amer Al-Murrah had been the premier tracker. He was able to decipher if a woman was pregnant from her footprint or the colour of an animal by its dung. But after he received the white truck he never tracked another missing person or thief or pregnant woman and never stopped when it wasn't necessary. It took some time to get the hang of steering, but direction was quickly becoming less important to the Al-Murrah than speed.

This massive exodus out of the desert and into the city occurred throughout the 1970s and nobody wore their seat-belts. In fact, so many family members had died terrible deaths or were badly maimed in accidents that when I returned alone to live with my extended family in Doha, I was convinced I'd meet my doom thrown through the windshield of some small sedan or under the wheel of a gravel truck. In the end, the aversion to being cloistered in our government-allocated borough and cockroach-infested house was greater than the aversion to being peeled off hot concrete.

My early memories of the Arabian Gulf are a heady mix of pearly-oil puddles, seat-belt rash and vomit. I was often sick and usually carsick. The roads of Abu Dhabi and Doha in the late 1980s were uneven or simply unfinished and the switch from burning heat to the frigid dry air of a rental car always sent me pale. A childhood spent riding in the back seat of fusty rental cars and being battened down on to the leather seats of the Scirocco was positively lavish when compared to the dog-pile strategy for seating used by my relations in Saudi. To them I was no hot-house flower bound and buckled into an ultra safety seat with matching helmet. The first time I visited, I was unnerved to find myself being herded with the rest of my twenty-three-plus cousins of comparable age into the back of a huge pea-green Suburban (or 'Al-Superman' as it was affectionately called) and driven deep into the desert to play cops and robbers and throw rocks at one another until late into the night. The freedom to squirm and climb and scream while on a long drive was dangerous and utterly liberating; I never wanted to get into Mother's comparatively tame Scirocco again.

Life on the receding and pockmarked Saudi roads was exciting and fun, with an endless and revolving set of playmates. We sang songs like 'Salamatek', a seat-belt-safety jingle, and ate Sindbad crisps. We drank buttermilk and got sunburned. But as I hit puberty I found myself discouraged from going on these road trips or riding in the front seat of a car. The reality of the situation began to cast heavy shadows on all my childhood pastimes and hobbies.

I could no longer wrestle with male cousins or visit my uncles in the men's sitting room. Running, jumping, climbing and, worst of all, swimming became taboo. Instead of cotton floral training bras, my wardrobe was invaded by sleeveless black 'training *abayas*' (black cloaks). I began to sympathize with Mother, who had been carless and jobless in our time there. She fought for her mobility and frequently suffered spurts of rebellion during which my sister and I would be toted into a taxi and driven to various spots along the beach or desert. She would tell the cab to stop at a jetty or dune and we would scramble over or around the obstruction and out of the cab driver's sight.

Her bravery and tempered defiance kept me afloat when I returned to the Gulf alone as a teenager and later as an adult.

Our last stint as a family unit in the Gulf ended messily. Father's second wife, who was not only seventeen but his cousin, came to make a social call. She knew that mother was aching to drive. And although houses, belongings and time are meant to be divvied out equally between the two wives, my father failed miserably at keeping both women sated. When Father left the room, his very pregnant second wife dangled her belly and his car keys in front of Mother's face. Wife number one calmly eyed the jangling keys as wife number two's chest swelled at her small triumph. She was not expecting the attack when my mother sprang at her. Wife number two crouched howling for their husband with the keys clutched to her swollen teats. Not realizing that the white woman was after the keys rather than wanting to murder her unborn child, she dropped the keys and rolled into the foetal position, still screaming and expecting a blow. Mother picked up the keys from the ruddy carpet and marched out the door, leaving wife number two confused and whimpering. We went to the American Embassy, where the ambassador obtained us three tickets home via London. My father was in no way holding us captive there, he was simply unaware of the pain that confinement was causing my mother. Within a day we were back on Grandmother's raspberry farm and bona fide born-again American women sudsing, rinsing and waxing the neglected Scirocco for action.

So it was that I came of American driving age while living in the Puget Sound, far from Qatar (where I couldn't legally drive before getting hitched) or Saudi, still home to most of our family (where I couldn't drive at all). On the wet and hilly roads of western Washington I was safe from the brutal traffic tragedies of desert highways. I just had to stick to defensive driving on our town's main drag. My first car was a Chevy El Camino. She was brown and beautiful, half car, half truck, and born the same year as I was. With her V8 engine and swooping, practical design, my cowboy Cadillac was more powerful and sleeker than any other car in town. The Korean kids had their Honda shopping carts with giant spoilers and the hillbillies had their souped-up GMC beaters, but none of them had a thing on the 'El'.

My best friend, Rita, invested in a Citizens' Band radio and public address system which was hooked up on to the dash. Rita stuck a huge holographic American flag sticker on to the dashboard which buckled and faded so badly by the end of the summer that it flaked right off. We wrote 'Cowboy Up!' in soap on the rear window and the thick CB antenna shot a good ten feet off the hood. And so we spent our teenage girlhood, flirting with truckers, carnies and roustabouts over the CB and harassing joggers over the PA. Despite the uncontrollable cool of the car, my sister still asked to be dropped off a block away from her junior high whenever I drove her to school.

We became known about town as the Mexican chicks with the truck car. It may not have helped that the 'El' had been modified with airbrushed purple flames and had 'Brown Pride' decaled on to the back window in Gothic Algerian script. But having grown up answering the question, 'Is Saddam yer dad?' being mistaken for Mexican was much easier than explaining the actual mottled source of our brownness. In fact, it was awesome.

It's been a decade since I drove the El Camino and almost as long since anyone's yelled *'mamacita'* (lil' mama) at me. I missed driving during the subsequent years living in the Gulf and Cairo, where I attended university. Very recently I received my Qatari driving licence from the High Traffic Council of the Emir. The rules had changed and now young women (twenty-four and up) could also obtain licence to peel out, burn rubber and four-wheel on the beach. In an act of spontaneous suffrage, my father decided the time had come for me to set up with the other ill-fated drivers of our clan. In reality he needed help trucking my seven brothers and sisters to and from school. I was thrilled at the prospect of driving again.

The High Traffic Council in Doha is Kafka's nightmare building. It is designed to look like a fascist structure of the future, as envisioned by a sightless architect in 1968. The doors are all flanked by at-ease guards and the corners of every room are rounded by mini-dunes of dust. After obtaining a dozen stamps from various Qatari officers, looking unnatural in their high-waisted uniforms, and posing for photographs of myself looking jaundiced in a tightly pulled veil, I emerged worn and totally unprepared for my eye examination.

A waddling officer took me to the women's entrance, upon which was scrawled the image of a single staring eye. My guide scratched his pantaloon, squeezed privates and told me to enter. I opened the Cyclops door, only to find myself pinned into a small broom closet, musty, unlit and full of a broken file cabinet. Squeezing past the cabinet, I found another door and emerged directly into the line of vision of a beaten-looking Indian man holding a piece of round tissue over his right eye and failing terribly at identifying the orientation of various 'E's which were now projected on to my long, black *abaya*. I skulked backwards into the closet and waited for a sign to re-enter. I practised focusing my eyes in the darkness to condition them for the test and swatted at what I thought were either cobwebs or the beginnings of a cataract. Despite this evidence that I was becoming blind and paranoid, I miraculously passed. The woman administering the test had me read a line of large numbers, asked if I normally wore contacts or a face veil, stamped my documents and sent me back the way I came.

This small triumph was tempered by the realization that motoring in Doha is so dangerous because no one bothers learning how to drive.

I had the Gulf at my wheel and nothing weighing on my mind but the prospect of flipping, skidding, being T-boned or flattened by a speeding Hummer, running into a lamp post or bursting into flames. I became the first female in our immediate family to get a driving licence, though non-Bedouin women have been driving Doha's streets for years now. The immobility of women in our tribe is ironic considering that they had cruised the Empty Quarter in Saudi long before city women had set foot outside their huts. And whenever my great-aunt Berkah tells her story of running away into the wilderness at fourteen in order to avoid her wedding night, receiving my licence to coast along the well-lit corniche and utilize valet parking seems something of an empty victory.

My fears were not assuaged by the dive-bomb attacks of young men on the roads near our home in Al-

Murrah City (the borough of Doha which is named after our tribe). There are several 'warring' gangs of long-haired, foul-mouthed, drag-racing young hoodlums who call themselves by the mascoted names of the 'Cops', the 'Terrorists' and, my personal favourite, the 'Mafia'. I have always been baffled as to why all of these gang names are spray-painted in English all over our neighbourhood.

The gangs are the singular obsession of my two youngest brothers. They spend hours pretending to be memorizing the Qur'an in the men's sitting room, when they are really drawing elaborate racing scenes with beautifully rendered Nissan pickups sporting decals of skulls and chequered racing flags and the bold printed words Mafia or Terrorists. All of these factions are from the larger tribe of Al-Murrah but are split into smaller groups by clan. The 'Terrorists', for instance, are the representatives of our clan. My father has forbidden my brothers from watching, although they are still part of a covert ring of boys who trade cell-phone videos via Bluetooth of Land Cruisers popping wheelies.

The newly paved road behind our house has recently become a favourite spot for late-night racing. The room my three brothers share and the room I share with my two sisters face the street, which is still unlit.

Although the lamp posts were erected months ago

they are standing unwired and looming in the darkness. Late into the night there is a buzzing audible in the distance. A swarm assembles at the gravelly end of the road where the pavement is unlaid. There in the west, towards Saudi, they rev their engines and the race begins. Black Toyota vs. White Nissan or Land Cruiser vs. Land Rover. The linchpin of the race is the traffic circle near our house.

It is the most dangerous part of the track.

A few roundabouts beyond ours is an adult-size rink of bumper cars. The fixture is rusty and would be quite threatening if it weren't for the jewelled automotive confections pinned in by its rubber kerbs. The roof of the rink is made of chicken wire and the rubber floor is slippery with sand. It has stood on an empty lot for at least three years and is guarded by a Filipino man in the evenings. Boys from the area flock to the rickety amusement and pay one riyal for five minutes of horseplay. Last week, I drove my half-brothers over the bumper stadium for their crash-and-burn rehearsal. The two had finished exams for their winter quarter and, with reserved lunch money in pocket, they begged to go. This was exactly the situation my father had anticipated my licence coming in handy for. The youngest, Salem, got in first, a canary-coloured cart, its lightning rod slightly bent at the middle. Meanwhile, Ali found a sleek black cart with the number seven stickered on to the side. The Filipino man was wresting a five-riyal note out of one of the older boys' hands when he flipped the electricity on. My brothers went hurtling around the rubber stage, aiming for one another, screeching threats and crashing with all their might. The clamour was almost done when the crooked pole attached to Salem's yellow car made a whinging noise and broke in half. The chicken wire ceiling showered Salem in sparks and the pole (no longer electrified) came crashing down in two pieces on either side of him. After a few moments of stunned silence the other boys carried on with their whizzing about. Salem was clearly frightened; he had speckled burns on his scalp and shoulders. We drove home buckled up and silent. On the way we passed a pickup carcass on the side of the road, belly up. There was no ambulance, just real policemen poking about the wreck.

As I dozed off that night I heard Salem crying into his mother's yielding arms. She was hushing him and promising him her usual promise: that he could have any car he wants when he is old enough. Early the next morning I was awakened by the sound of my stepmother weeping alone in the gravel out-side our house. Father was backing quickly out of the driveway just as the mosque's morning call-to-prayer began. My cousin Abdallah had been thrown from his truck in a collision with the median on the

Saudi–Qatar highway the night before. He had died while we slept.

Abdallah had been a star among his many brothers and was considered a catch by all the girls in our clan: he had been handsome, smart, religious and kind. Four traits not easily found in one prospect. He'd been engaged a few times before they had always fallen through for inexplicable reasons. A few weeks before his death he had been properly betrothed to a cousin. The weekend of his death he had gone to Saudi to buy sequined sundries and perfume for his fiancée's trousseau. Abdallah had called his future wife just moments before his collision and told her he'd drop off the presents in a few minutes.

It was his unmarried widow who had alerted Abdallah's mother when he didn't show up. By all accounts he was the happiest he'd ever been while readying himself for the joys and possibility of this long-overdue love.

On the night of the accident, Fatma, Abdallah's eldest sister, had been admitted to Hamad General Hospital. She was over nine months pregnant at this point. Her baby was still clinging stubbornly to the shaded darkness of her womb, biding his time amidst the feathery sway of placenta and amniotic fluid. But the peaceful silence inside of Fatma's body was not to last. Her water broke when she heard the traumatic news of her brother's death.

Borne in on a thin stretcher from the highway's sandy margin, Abdallah was suffering from severe internal bleeding and broken bones. There was no external wound but for a crack across the top of his skull and forehead where he had landed several metres from his crumpled truck. Abdallah's father informed us that he had looked peaceful before he passed away in the hospital. At the moment of Abdallah's death his mother and sister were just a floor above him. His last faint breath dissipated into the fluorescent lights just as Fatma heaved her reluctant child from her body.

That early morning before either the newly dead or the newly born had been removed from the hospital premises, Bakhita, the bereaved mother and thrilled grandmother, pointed out the strange purple birthmark which ran over the infant's pinking scalp to his wrinkled little forehead. Everyone marvelled at the miracle: '*SubhanAllah*.' (God is great.)

Of course, they named him Abdallah.

Even after Abdallah's tragic death, the drag races haven't stopped. My little brothers still wait up in the dark and hang themselves out of their open window.

Squatting on the windowsill, they silently wave and muffle their cheers as the Mafia zoom by and tip at the roundabout. Salem seems to be recovered from his bumper-car fright; he even suggested returning before the vacation is over to see if his yellow cart is back in order. The cannonade of backfires and screeches outside our windows every night has him in a frenzy to get behind a wheel – any wheel – as quickly as possible. The initial disapproval which had stung all talk of cars between my brothers and my father following Abdallah's death has begun to fade as my eldest half-sibling, Aziz, prepares to get his own driving licence. The feuding Cops and Terrorists swivel at the roundabout and go tumbling back towards the Saudi border. Every night we hear honking and see red lights in the distance, but we never find out who won the race.

Mothers and Daughters

Jenneba Sie-Jalloh

I come from a family who love telling stories. Embellishment is a way of life. My mother is Irish and I believe the Irish story-telling tradition has been a huge influence on me. My father, from Sierra Leone, also liked to tell stories.

As a child my mother told me stories about her childhood and family in Ireland. I knew all about family feuds, secrets and eccentricities. Somewhere along the line, I believe, it inspired me to write.

My mother continues to inspire me and we still share interesting times together . . .

My mother calls with a proposal: 'It's called "Self-awareness and Confidence-building for Irish Women". It's my fourth time. I want you to come with me.'

'Why?'

'Because I do. It's very interesting and I'd like you to come.'

'I'm not Irish.'

'I'm your mother and *I'm* Irish.'

'I'd feel like a fraud.'

'You think someone's going to tell you to leave?'

I shudder.

'They'd have to get rid of me too.'

The phone slips a little in my hand. Oh, God, possible confrontation. Even worse.

'You're my daughter, aren't you?'

I nod for my own comfort.

'You come from me, don't you?'

All true. It was settled. I was going.

The following Thursday morning I meet my mother at 9.00 a.m. This means we will be approximately forty-five minutes early for the meeting, but I resist the temptation to mention it.

As I didn't have time to unplait my hair, I've scooped the whole bunch up into a clapped-out hairband at the nape of my neck. My mother beams when she sees me and stretches out her hand to touch my shoulder.

'You look lovely.' She stops smiling and starts walking. 'You'll do.'

We cross Tavistock Road and wait for the number 328 bus outside Westbourne Park Station. At Kilburn High Road, we get off the bus behind an elderly woman who's having trouble negotiating an empty shopping trolley. Her small thin frame is bent and wrapped around the trolley rather like a mature vine around a gatepost. My mother helps with a corner of the trolley and the woman turns around and smiles at her. My mother sees this as an opportunity to enter into full conversation with the woman, as if the plan all along was to meet here, on this spot of pavement, in order to discuss the pros and cons of hip replacements.

We talk for ten minutes. I refrain from nudging or clearing my throat theatrically. This is my mother's morning. I have given it over to her and I will be a patient, cheerful and magnanimous daughter, whatever happens.

Finally my mother assures the woman that the doctors at St Mary's Hospital, Paddington, are the best in the world.

'They know what they're doing. My daughter and my grandson were both born there, couldn't be healthier. The operation will be a success and you'll be as right as rain!'

Just before my resolve runs out, I glance over my mother's body, deciding on which bit to poke without drawing attention. She gently pats the woman on the back.

'God bless now.' My mother turns to me. 'Didn't have the heart to tell her that I don't trust a single doctor anywhere.'

I give her a disapproving look.

My mother says, 'She's eighty-six. What's she got to lose?' She looks down at her watch. 'Ah, look at that. We're early! We might as well go into the church.'

I breathe in and say quietly on my out breath, 'It's your morning. Make the most of it.'

But it counts for nothing. She's already four steps ahead of me, striding up the gravel courtyard towards the Church of Our Lady of Sorrow.

As we enter the huge brown door, I make a connection with the white marble statue of a tortured St Catherine, wheel at her feet, staring down at us. We've arrived in the middle of the Mass. The priest is standing at the altar, his arms stretched towards us. I am on familiar territory.

'Pray for all those who are lonely or depressed. Lord hear us . . .'

As I watch the elderly priest say Mass I remember the words of my Syrian cab driver the week before.

He asks me where I'm from and I answer, Ladbroke Grove, before telling him what he really wants to know.

'I'm Irish-African.'

'Ah.'

'My mum and dad met at Paddington Station, fifty years ago. My dad's Muslim.'

I like to make connections where I can.

The driver looks pleased, then sad.

After an impassioned yet friendly discussion about

the wearing of the veil, in which I offer my own sartorial philosophy – 'I like clothes that make me smile' – the driver fixes his eyes on me via his rear-view mirror and says, 'If you have one Muslim parent, you too are Muslim.'

I am taken aback, surprised and delighted. I am being claimed – unconditionally. It feels unfamiliar. It feels good and right, like standing here now, in the church, with my mother.

'Lord, graciously hear us.'

I mouth the words, without thinking, along with the rest of the congregation.

My mother points at the small stone font next to me. Again, without thinking, I dip my index finger into the cool water and cross myself with the tip of my finger: forehead, chest, left shoulder, right shoulder, lips. Automatic. Comforting. My mother touches my finger with her own, then puts it to her forehead and crosses herself with what's left of the water, which is barely a trace. This seems to satisfy her and, strangely, it satisfies me too.

My mother whispers to me across the font, 'Let's go before we're late.'

I want to tell her that it's impossible to be late but instead follow, without a word, out of the church, toward West Hampstead, or the back of Kilburn, depending on which way you look at it.

We arrive at the centre. The meeting is held in a small, airy room at the back of the building. The room smells of tea. There are eight women, average age of sixty, sitting in a circle. Their eyes turn to me as we enter the room. My shoulders tighten. I force some movement around the corners of my mouth. I feel like a small brown speckled fish whipped out of my pond and cast into an unpredictable green sea. Why did I come? I knew from the start it was a mistake. My mother, on the other hand, is oblivious to the situation: the staring, my discomfort. In fact, I can feel her body next to mine, twitching with excitement.

'This is my daughter . . .' She grabs my arm, which is difficult because we're standing so close, as if I'm about to run. 'She has come with me just for today, for support.'

Support? I'm here under false pretences. I shouldn't even be here. It's a closed group! I wriggle my arm in her grip to show my dissatisfaction. My mother finishes her introduction and smiles at me, squeezing my arm lovingly in return. She's having a ball: an audience and a prisoner.

I scan the faces of the women. I try to gauge their expression. Bemused and curious, I decide, but not hostile.

There's an air of melancholy in the room suffused with good humour as one by one the women recount their tales from the week. The highs and lows of daughters and sons, husbands and loneliness. Laughter permeates the plentiful nods and shaking of heads, the frowns and words of encouragement.

It's my mother's turn to talk next and I feel nervous again. I know for a fact that I have featured at least once during her week, and not necessarily in a good way. I have to give credit to her as, tactfully, she is careful not to mention me during her recap. However, she still manages to talk more than anyone else. Again, I steel myself, keep my head down and resist the temptation to give her a look or a nudge.

It's her gig.

My turn next.

I swallow. I say, shyly, that's it's been a good week with the occasional down and leave it at that. The women nod and smile approvingly. Everyone is relieved.

There are few situations as revealing as watching your mother interacting with people you don't know, in an unfamiliar environment. Witnessing the similarities between you is startling. Perhaps that's why mothers and daughters clash when they do. They're vying for the same space. Seeking to inhabit the same spot, whether they like it or not. Needlessly at loggerheads, when the truth is, the world is full of space. More room than either of them could imagine or wish for.

The meeting comes to an end. The women look relaxed. A load, or at least a couple of packages, have been lifted. Gráinne, the young coordinator, offers us all tea in the back room. My mother stands up as if the fire alarm has been sounded and reaches for her bag. I wonder why she needs one so big, as there's barely anything in it.

'We'll go on now, Gráinne.'

'Sure you won't have a cup of tea now ... and a bun?'

My mother looks at me and hesitates.

'No. We'll be off. Things to do.'

I'm hoping that's a nicety or wishful thinking on my mother's part.

'That's grand.' Gráinne smiles at me. 'It's been lovely having you. Come back again, won't you.'

I'd love to, I say. We both know it's unlikely, but the sentiment is real.

As we walk into the bold October sunshine my mother, encouraged by the success of the expedition, turns to me and announces, 'There's a film on the week after next at the Irish Centre in Hammer-smith ...'

She pauses. I don't respond.

She continues, 'It's called, *I Only Came over for a Couple of Years*. What do you think?'

I think she's pushing her luck. I don't answer straight away. I think about my little Westbourne

Park pond and the big old sea: my mother's world and mine. Different waters.

We walk with the sun on our faces and I feel it warming my chest and cheeks.

'I think –' I turn to my mother and notice the small deep lines gathered like fine stitches around the corners of her mouth and the flecks of green in her eyes – 'that, that sounds like it might be interesting.'

She smiles. We turn the corner at the end of Quex Road into the busy brightness of Kilburn High Road, content in our own close and singular way.

The Amruthur Iyengar Family

Radhika Praveen

If you have lived in a city that is a tangle of cultures like Mumbai for as long as twenty-seven years, you find that you can no longer mark on the threads where the differences begin or the similarities end. You just learn to weave them together into the fabric of your life and wear it wherever you go, shining in the brilliance of their contrasts, their colours and texture. The more you expose this cloth, this second skin to the world, the more patterns it takes on itself, a garden of embroidery forever growing, forever changing, that smells of whole-hearted love, of sunlit childhood memories and, of course, of food.

I can still hear the short, sharp bursts of their carefree laughter from the kitchen over the whistling pressure cooker, the knife running through a cushion of steaming Gujarati *dhokla* on a wide round plate, batches of fast-fluffing-up *puris* in oil, hot Rajasthani *gatte-ki-sabji* being spooned out into bowls, the spluttering mustard and cumin seeds, and peanuts that will go into spicy golden Iyengar *puliyogare* and Iyer *thairchadam*. A Maharashtrian *shrikhand* box is opened with a pop, while shiny stainless-steel plates and glasses are being arranged on the floor, for three generations at a family get-together.

The oldest member in the house, seated huddled by the wall as always, is *amma*. Despite the half-set of dentures in her mouth, a face chiselled by the years of hurt and anger, of losses of lives and relationships, she laughs loudest, a sudden, contagious laughter. There are but tiny joys that survive in her life – among which is an obsession for the local daily news on TV, Kit-Kat chocolate bars and vanilla ice cream. Most of all, she sports an eighty-plus-year-old pride that grows more stubborn with every coughing fit.

Come here, she beckons with a nod of the head, *and sit next to me*, with another. I smile and obey. I know this is going to take a long time. My grandmother prefers to live by herself and is fiercely protective of her independence in the small one-room apartment where she has stayed for over twenty-five years. Yet every time we meet, she can't resist narrating the story of her life to anyone willing to listen. I sit close to her, drawing patterns on her wrinkled skin, which seems to shrink and expand with amazing elasticity.

Iyengar Puliyogare

Cook 2 cups rice with a pinch of turmeric added to the water. Set this cooked yellow rice aside to cool. Roast separately 3:1:½ parts coriander seeds, cumin seeds and fenugreek seeds, 10–15 dried red chillies or according to taste, and grind them together. Use a lemon-sized ball of tamarind and squeeze it under water in a bowl. Heat the tamarind water and mix the powders in till the amount of water is reduced to half and the paste starts bubbling and splashing about. (Alternatively, 2–3 spoons of the tamarind concentrate can be used. Mix the powders well with this paste.) This paste can also be preserved in the fridge for a month.

Pour over the cooked rice. Season some oil with mustard seeds and cumin seeds, a lot of curry leaves, redskin peanuts, salt, and 1 or 2 dried red chillies. Pour this over the paste and rice, and mix well. Garnish with dried, sliced coconut and roasted sesame seeds. Serves 4.

Saroja and her five children belonged to the Iyengar community that came from the Amruthur village in Bangalore, Karnataka. Well known for their *puliyogare*, and feared for their rather orthodox and conservative way of life, the community, in the 1930s, was not very kind to this fourth daughter of a poor village schoolteacher, who withdrew her from school and assigned her to menial jobs around the house. Uneducated, unwanted, she was married off to a small-time tailor with very little income to raise four young girl children. He left for Bombay (now known as Mumbai) in search of better prospects, leaving Saroja and the kids with her mother in the village. In time, he did find a job, and a tiny, one-room apartment in a Bombay suburb, and called the family over. Soon the fifth child, a son, was also born. When the boy was three, after dinner one evening, Saroja's husband died of cardiac arrest.

The two older just-graduated daughters soon found themselves working as receptionists, or clerks, in offices and bringing home a meagre salary. The third helped by providing home tuition. As years passed, jobs and fortunes changed, the three of them found their life partners where they worked. The fourth sister, who was studying in college then, also found a classmate with whom she wanted to spend her life.

Gujarati Dhokla

Dals, soaked in advance for 6–8 hours: 1 cup – tur dal, chana dal (pigeon peas, yellow gram dal); half-cup mung and urad dals. Grind these coarsely with yoghurt, mix with 2 cups of rice flour and let the batter rest overnight. Add ginger and chilli paste, turmeric and salt to the mixture the next day. Heat a little oil, adding a pinch of baking powder. When it bubbles, add this to the batter and stir well.

Grease a round stainless-steel plate and pour the batter on to it. Place over a wok with a little boiling water. Ensure that the water doesn't get on to the plate. Cover and leave it to simmer for 8–10 minutes. When it has cooled, cut into squares and sandwich them together with a coriander chutney or dip. Finally, arrange these in a plate and, to garnish, season with mustard seeds, 1 or 2 split chillies (optional), sesame seeds, some chopped coriander and grated coconut. Serves 4–6.

Indian Hindu families consider it a prime duty to marry off their girls into families from the same caste and above their social status, and boys to families below the same. But Saroja, who was entirely dependent on her children, with no source of income, had no option but to humbly accept her daughters' inter-caste, inter-cultural choices.

And so, the Iyengar family branched out: the eldest sister – my mother – married a Malayali from Kerala. My three *chittis* (maternal aunts) married a Gujarati from Surendranagar in Gujarat, a Marwari from Rajasthan and a Tamilian from the Iyer community respectively. You must understand that despite the fact that all these were marriages by choice, each of them had to face at least some reluctance from their spouses' joint and extended families, even banishment from the community.

Rajasthani Gatte-ki-sabji
Make a dough with 1 cup gram flour, buttermilk, powdered fennel seeds, garam masala or curry powder, turmeric and salt, and shape into cylinders. Steam these and, when they are done, slice them into rings. In a kadhai or wok, season with mustard and cumin seeds, chillies to taste, chopped onions and tomatoes, and roast until they make a pulpy and fragrant curry base. Add

the sliced rings to this (some prefer frying the steamed rings before adding them here), garnish with some lemon and chopped coriander, and serve hot with rotis or puris. *Serves 2.*

When the last and only brother fell in love, he brought home a Maharashtrian wife. This time, my grandmother opposed the wedding. Being the only son, who would carry forward the Iyengar name, she couldn't bear to see him spend the rest of his life with a Maharashtrian widow who already had a child from her first marriage. I still recall her desperate cries and pleas, asking her helpless sons-in-law and daughters to stop this union, which she believed was inauspicious. But my uncle was determined.

A small wedding soon took place, with very little ceremony, the sisters and their families, a sulking mother and even fewer friends. I remember that as children we were quite excited about the event ... A Marathi *mami* had joined the family and we even had a new cousin!

Those were the days ... My grandmother sighs, blinking her dull eyes that are flooded with tears, and wriggles her fingers from the hands clasped around her skinny, huddled-together knees, unable to talk any more. I rub her back, as I always do when she ends the story at this point, reminding her she should be happy that at least we are all together now. Thankfully, lunch is served and we sit down to eat.

Maharashtrian Shrikhand

Leave a pot of plain yoghurt in a cheesecloth-lined strainer in the refrigerator overnight, or for 6–8 hours. Add 3–4 tablespoons of sugar, a little at a time, to the strained yoghurt, stirring all the time. When all the sugar has been dissolved, add saffron that has been soaked in a little warm milk, and garnish with coarsely chopped pistachios and other nuts. The amount of sugar can be altered according to taste, or calories. Enjoy chilled, with puris, or as a simple sweet dish after dinner.

In Mumbai, nobody has the time to brood over sour relationships. And every Indian heart believes that Time is the best healer of all.

For the five Iyengar siblings, when their children were born, one by one, they brought together all the loose threads. They restored the injured pride and egos with laughter and innocent cackles that echoed back home in all their families. The multicultural fabric of the Amruthur Iyengar family began to assimilate colours and flutter again.

Ten cousins. We grew up together, under five different roofs, united not only by love, blood and religion, but also, strangely, by our many mother tongues, the foods, the quarrels, Bollywood films, and the common Hindi and Marathi language that we all used to communicate in. We always looked forward to the school vacations, when we stayed over at each other's places, helping our mothers lay out mangoes for pickling on the terrace, or *papads* (poppadoms) to dry under the sun. We played, read and exchanged picture books, and simply ate till we thought we would burst. And there were the festivals, when we could do all fun things at once.

Naive and snug inside the stronghold of my maternal connections, I did not once believe that I was in fact missing what my father's family back in Kerala would have to offer, had I been as close to my cousins in the south of India as well. It was never a deliberate oversight, but when I now hear about Kerala's rich literature, the legacy of stories and secrets in my father's ancestral home, I cannot help feeling a tinge of regret. Perhaps my father had a taste of this isolation too when he left for Bombay at the age of sixteen, before he finally got used to it.

Our visits to my father's home town were rare. And when we did travel down south, we were very fond of but couldn't always relate to our Malayali cousins. They made fun of the way we spoke their language and the skirts we wore that revealed our dark and rough knees. In one word, we were Outsiders. Although we never displayed it openly, I think there might have also been an undercurrent of city girls vs. small-town cousins tug-of-war. By the time we forgot about this war, by the time we were playing unconditionally like blood relatives should, the vacation was over and we had to leave.

Dessert: Kerala Parippu Pradhaman

Roast a cup of yellow mung dal until browned. Cook the roasted dal in a pressure cooker till they are soft. Add half a cup of jaggery and half a can of thick coconut milk to the cooked dal, and keep stirring on a slow flame. When the jaggery has all melted, add some powdered cardamom, and about ¼ cup of diluted coconut milk. Take it off the heat. Garnish with cashew nuts and raisins browned in a spoonful of hot ghee. Serves 4.

Imagine Europe to be one big country, with its varied cultures, people and their many foods and languages. India is one such vast country. There are twenty-eight states in India and about twenty-nine major languages are spoken by more than a million native speakers; 122 languages are spoken by more than 10,000, according to the country's latest 2001 census report. There are other individual Indian mother tongues that number several hundred.

Where we lived, there were thirteen flats. We Keralites were surrounded by Maharashtrian, Andhra and Punjabi neighbours, with whom we loved to exchange and share our food. We went to an English-language school, where we had Hindu, Muslim and Christian friends. We ended up being more fluent in Hindi and Marathi, spoke Malayalam and English in the house, and understood the Tamil and Kannada languages that my grandmother switched to from

Hindi when she had some secret information to share with her daughters.

In time, my Gujarati cousins were married off into well-respected Gujarati families. My Marwari sister married an Agarwal from the same community. My Kerala-Iyer cousin chose to marry a Maharashtrian girl he had been courting for five years. My paternal cousin married a Punjabi colleague and took her to the US, where they live happily with their two children. His sister's marriage was arranged with a well-settled, decent Malayali boy from a traditional family background. Next, it would be my younger sister or me any time . . .

With such a résumé of mixed-culture marriages, my mother often worried: would we girls be happy in a purely Nair non-vegetarian household? Would we be able to chop heads off chickens and fish, like we cut our humble *bhindi* and *batata* (okra and potato)?

She needn't have. My sister, who went trekking up the Himalayas, chose a Gujarati boy from her mountaineering group. The boy's family had been based in Chennai, southern India, for three generations, and they lived in a purely vegetarian, joint-family household of at least sixteen members spread over two homes in the same building. After four years of distant courtship, they were finally married.

In an already huge and full house, decked from

head to toe in new clothes and jewellery, my sister remembers spending the first day in her new home sporting a big smile – in front of at least fifty unfamiliar faces who had come to see her. Later, she would learn that here was a way of life quite unlike our own – family business was topmost on the list of all the men in her husband's house; everything else was secondary. The women did the PR, concentrating on maintaining good terms with extended family members who were spread all over India. They kept themselves abreast of any new developments (a marriage somewhere, a baby on the way) or gossip, and warmly entertained guests who arrived to stay with them.

Iyer Thairchadam (Yoghurt Rice)
Mix 2 cups of leftover, cooked plain rice with cold, fresh yoghurt, grated cucumber and salt. Season with mustard seeds and cumin seeds, curry leaves, some asafoetida or hing, diced ginger and a hint of garlic. Serves 3–4. (Leftover rice works best for this dish, which cools and is refreshing to have on any long day or after a spicy puliyogare.)

I arrived in London on a cold December 2001 evening, a month after my marriage. It was my first trip abroad. The only England I knew – the 'Raj' from my school history books that ruled over India and colonized half the world, and the 'foreign' Eng-land, where Bollywood actors often burst into songs and dance in front of visibly amused British onlookers – was to be my new home.

My Iyer husband had already been working here for two years, so his friends became my friends. I didn't know anybody else, but I was curious for more.

Dressed in new *salwar kameez* sets like any new Indian bride, I shivered under an ugly lumpy coat that all but failed to keep me warm and tangled my hair instead. Each day, after my husband left for the office, I would set out alone, visiting the big library at the town centre, taking the H9 to his IT office, which was based at scenic Harefield village. I travelled on the tube and once ended up on the wrong bus that took me to Shepherd's Bush instead of Uxbridge station. Before I knew it, within two weeks of my arrival in London, one Sunday morning I collapsed.

When I opened my eyes weakly, I saw a handsome Greek doctor extracting some of my blood into a couple of frightening syringes while my husband looked on, very worried. We were told it was a simple case of low blood pressure and dehydration, thanks to complete lack of preparation for the cold English climate, while a Caribbean and a Malaysian nurse took turns changing the saline drips. Soon I had completely recovered, when another nurse, Filipino this time, came to take my details for the last time.

Nurse: What is your name?
Me: Radhika.
Nurse: Is that your Christian name?
Me (surprised, almost hurt by his question): No. It is my Hindu name.

At this point my husband burst into laughter, startling both of us. He explained, first to me, that the nurse had meant to ask if 'Radhika' was my *first* name, and, then to him, that I was a new entrant to the UK, that Indians attach a lot of significance to their names and their meanings, and that I hadn't understood his question in the first place. It lightened up the whole situation at once, and there began my education about living in a new country.

I learned that brown people were to be classified as 'Asian' and not Indian or Pakistani. Close to our house, Polish and Punjabi workers stood side by side, mixing cement or simply taking a cigarette break. At a small one-time stint in a beauty parlour in Southall, I applied Gujarati-style, bridal henna on the palms of a fair young woman who was to travel to a family wedding in the US. We exchanged our stories over that half-hour, and I was thrilled, secretly, that while Indians and Pakistanis were fighting alongside their borders, here I was, happily chatting and holding hands with someone from 'the other side'. I called my mother in India and shouted out to her, excited: 'London is the new Mumbai'.

When I think of my mixed heritage, I often feel nostalgic about our family get-togethers and my cousins, who are all settled in India and in different places around the world: Chennai, Mumbai, Australia, US, London. I am reminded of my grandmother Saroja's story about when she first travelled to Bombay with her four children. I look at my own little one then and wonder where life will take him.

In contrast to the mixed cousins that I grew up with, my son plays all by himself and settles down easily in front of *CBeebies* on TV. I recognize and understand the extended family that is already his. *The Tweenies*, IgglePiggle with his tinkling red blanket, *RazzleDazzle*, Sportacus from *LazyTown*, the friends from *Balamory*, the *Story Makers* and the Blue Cow. He talks to them and they keep him entertained, in their British-accented English. We talk to him in Tamil, because he has Iyer roots, and that is his father's language. My parents – over the phone or the Internet – talk to him in Malayalam. My husband and I speak Hindi at home and also in front of him. Our Maharashtrian friends converse with him strictly in Marathi. My sixteen-month-old, I hope, understands all these languages.

English Jacket Potatoes
Wash potatoes (the bigger, the better) and dry them thoroughly. Next, prick the skins a few times with a fork, then put a few

drops of olive oil over each one and rub it all over the skin. Rub in some crushed salt. Place the potatoes straight on to the centre shelf of a hot oven and let them bake for two hours, or until the skins are really crisp.

Slit each potato in half lengthways and top with the butter and seasoning. Serve immediately with a filling of choice.

For two days a week, we let our son stay away from the only people he knows and mingle instead with eighteen other children of his age at a nursery not far from home. We don't know these other kids, and where and which nationalities they belong to. But in multicultural London, this is the upbringing we have chosen for him. Just like my parents did, when they travelled to a similarly diverse Bombay in their youth, wishing to give us the best upbringing they could.

One day, my son might ask us who he really is, where we come from, or why we are here and not with his grandparents in India. Until we have the answer, we will wrap our multicoloured, thickly woven and rich, patterned fabric around him like a warm winter jacket, with the smell of delicious, home-cooked food still clinging to it.

Notes on the Authors

Rashid Adamson

I am thirty-eight years old. Five years ago I left prison and almost got straight back into the habit that took me there in the first place: cocaine. However, miraculously, from a dark place a bright light shone and I began to trust my instincts and believe in myself. Childhood circumstance prevented me from obtaining an education when I was younger. I am now, thanks to hard work and determination, finishing my second year of a BA Joint Honours Degree in Creative Writing and Journalism at the University of Cumbria.

Sethina Adjarewa

I am the mother of two lovely daughters, Jasmine and Jada, who keep me entertained and busy. Having left Accra in 1973, I now live in Bristol, where I am studying medicine. I expect to graduate as a doctor a few months after my fortieth birthday in 2010.

I decided to become a doctor after the birth of my first child, leaving a career in marketing and public relations. I have never returned to Ghana, but hope to complete a medical elective there in 2009.

Sophia Al-Maria

I am a writer and ragamuffin living in south-east London. Previously I was a video editor in New York City, a student of pre-Islamic poetry in Cairo, a budding adolescent in the Arabian Gulf and a foetus in Tacoma, Washington.

Julia Bohanna

I was born an undersized baby in Newport, Gwent, and grew up in a Victorian house on the river in the wonderful but at the time unenlightened town of Hereford. I now work as a writer for the UK Wolf Conservation Trust's magazine, *Wolfprint*. I have also had some short stories published (in, for example, *Mslexia*) and some success in writing competitions (winner of the *Woman and Home* Short Story Competition in 2006). I live in Caversham, Berkshire, with a film model-maker and one ten-year-old daughter. Cats and chickens too.

Rounke Coker

Born in 1962 of mixed parentage, I grew up in a nuclear family of four, with many English ways of doing things. But I had a very large African extended family living and working just down the road in Lagos, Nigeria. I now live in shared accommodation in Brighton, southern England, where I initially came to do postgraduate work in Development Studies. I work as a resources assistant in an academic library, where my interest in the development of humorous situations through cultural misunderstanding continues to be engaged. 'Rounke Coker' is a pseudonym.

Fay Dickinson

I was born in Market Harborough in 1960. My English mother came from Hinckley, Leicestershire, and my Anglo-Indian father was originally from Lucknow. In 1985 I graduated from the University of Lancaster with a degree in English. My varied employment CV includes Keep Corby Tidy project worker, secretary and quality manager. Currently I'm a part-time accounts assistant. I live with my mother in Corby, Northamptonshire, and have one brother, who was born in 1963. I jokingly describe myself as part English, part Asian and part mad . . .

Claire Frank

I grew up in Suffolk but had no idea that one day I would spend most of my life on a Caribbean island. I went to live in Barbuda with my husband, who had always wanted to return after leaving on a boat when he was eight. We took our two small daughters and then my son was born and I started to write about their experiences of a life that spans two cultures. Several years of horrendously expensive long-haul travel and separation later, we are back in the UK for secondary school – but the day they all leave I will go back.

Tina Freeth

I decided that I wanted to write in 2006, when I produced my first piece of creative non-fiction, 'Growing up on Lard'. I wrote about what I knew, which happened to be about me eating a lot of unhealthy food and being sort of Chinese and sort of English. I am the first British Chinese student on the National

Academy of Writing course in Birmingham and one of the winners of the BBC Bites screenwriting competition. I have had a couple of short stories published – both with food appearing as a theme. I'm currently working on an autobiography, which will include how I discovered my biological father who is a tai chi master and lives just thirty minutes away!

Bel Greenwood

Born in London, I spent years travelling before living on Dartmoor and moving to Norfolk to do the Creative Writing MA at the University of East Anglia. Now I write scripts, play the accordion incredibly badly and bring up my beautiful daughter.

John A. Pitts

I enjoy the challenge of trying to transfer thoughts through words, music and photography, and then sharing them in a way that helps other people connect with my view of the world. While my writing is a very personal, almost self-indulgent journey, my goal is to use it to make the rest of the world want to hitch a ride with me every now and then! Born and raised in Sheffield, I now live in north London with my girlfriend, Keziah, and play in the band Bare Knuckle Soul.

Radhika Praveen

I was born in Mumbai and lived my first twenty-seven years there, feeding on *Amar Chitra Kathas* and the *Time* and *Life* magazines that I always found in my father's briefcase. At twenty-one, I was ploughing through dense technology jargon as a copy-editor at various IT publications. Four years later, desperate for the sound of simple words again, I began an online journal, where I still write, off and on. In 2007 I completed an MA in Professional Writing at London Metropolitan University and, at thirty-three now, done with over a decade of IT editing, I am enrolled for a PhD and working on my first novel.

Monika-Akila Richards

My first birth names are Monika and Georgia and I was born close to Hamburg. In my childhood most people called me Moni, which is now reserved only for family and old friends. In my teenage years, seeking to belong, I called myself Georgia. This was a big nod to black America, its music, Afro hairstyles and the civil rights movement. When I lived abroad and finally settled in England, my experience with the Rasta faith and black communities and the exploration of my African heritage helped me to discover Akila. I now choose to represent both my German and my African heritage in my name.

Kristyan Robinson

I was born in 1963 in London, Ontario, Canada. I've worked as an actress, musician and artist, as well as a fork-lift truck driver and a legal secretary. I've lived in London, England, since 1989. In September 2007 I graduated with a BA in Fine Arts from Goldsmiths, University of London. Throughout my studies I found myself continually wrestling with the tension between text and image. If the work of the visual artist is to make images, then perhaps writing is the most effective medium, for the images generated in the mind of the reader through the act of reading are long-lasting and personal.

Jennebah Sie-Jalloh

I was born and raised in Paddington and Notting Hill, west London, where I still live. I was born in 1964, the year of the first Notting Hill Carnival, and always make it back from wherever I am to be a part of it, if only to sit on my step and watch it all go by. My mother is from Dublin, my father from Sierra Leone. I am a teacher by profession and taught in Peckham for six years before moving into arts education. I live with my seventeen-year-old son; my mother lives round the corner! I have just completed an MA in Fiction and am working on my first novel.

He just wanted a decent book to read ...

Not too much to ask, is it? It was in 1935 when Allen Lane, Managing Director of Bodley Head Publishers, stood on a platform at Exeter railway station looking for something good to read on his journey back to London. His choice was limited to popular magazines and poor-quality paperbacks – the same choice faced every day by the vast majority of readers, few of whom could afford hardbacks. Lane's disappointment and subsequent anger at the range of books generally available led him to found a company – and change the world.

'We believed in the existence in this country of a vast reading public for intelligent books at a low price, and staked everything on it'
Sir Allen Lane, 1902–1970, founder of Penguin Books

The quality paperback had arrived – and not just in bookshops. Lane was adamant that his Penguins should appear in chain stores and tobacconists, and should cost no more than a packet of cigarettes.

Reading habits (and cigarette prices) have changed since 1935, but Penguin still believes in publishing the best books for everybody to enjoy. We still believe that good design costs no more than bad design, and we still believe that quality books published passionately and responsibly make the world a better place.

So wherever you see the little bird – whether it's on a piece of prize-winning literary fiction or a celebrity autobiography, political tour de force or historical masterpiece, a serial-killer thriller, reference book, world classic or a piece of pure escapism – you can bet that it represents the very best that the genre has to offer.

Whatever you like to read – trust Penguin.